The War
We Could Have Lost

The American Revolution

BY THE SAME AUTHOR

*Devil's Shadow: The Story of Witchcraft in
Massachusetts*

*Gathering Storm: The Story of the Green
Mountain Boys*

Osceola & the Seminole Wars

*Royal Opposition: The British Generals
in the American Revolution*

Story of the Thirteen Colonies

The War
We Could Have Lost

The American Revolution

CLIFFORD LINDSEY ALDERMAN

Four Winds Press New York

Published by Four Winds Press
A Division of Scholastic Magazines, Inc., New York, N.Y.
Copyright © 1974 by Clifford Lindsey Alderman

Printed in the United States of America
Library of Congress Catalog Card Number: 74–8334

LIBRARY OF CONGRESS CATALOGING IN PUBLICATION DATA
Alderman, Clifford Lindsey.   The war we could have lost.
   SUMMARY: A discussion of the American Revolution
which investigates the succession of British blunders
and emphasizes the heavy odds against American success.
   1.   United States—History—Revolution, 1775–1783—
Juvenile literature.   [1.   United States—History—
Revolution, 1775–1783]   I.   Title.   E208.A387
973.3'3   74–8334   ISBN 0–590–07300–1

Title page photo — courtesy of the New York Public Library Picture Collection.

For aspiring young author
Stacy Wishnak

Contents

1   Why We Could Have Lost the American Revolution   1

2   Not-So-Mighty Ticonderoga   6

3   The Rabble in Arms   16

4   Charleston, 1776, a Hornets' Nest   28

5   Howe Wins and Loses on Long Island   37

6   Manhattan and the Interrupted Chase   47

7   The Dilatory Dogs of War and the Slippery Fox   58

8   Burgoyne Makes His First Mistake   64

9   Burgoyne's Second Mistake   75

10   "Hangs Like a Gathering Storm . . ."   87

11   And Howe, Oh, Where Was He?   99

12   Bloody Footprints in the Snow   111

13   The British Turn South   127

14   Clinton's Revenge   138

15   Cowardice at Camden   146

16 A Pale Dawn Glimmers   158

17 Cowpens and the Chase toward Ruin   172

18 Cornwallis' Last Long Road   185

19 The British Government Culprits   201

Bibliography   210

Suggested Further Reading   217

Index   219

The War
We Could Have Lost
The American Revolution

1

Why We Could Have Lost the American Revolution

THE MORE ONE STUDIES THE AMERICAN REVOLUTION THE more incredible it seems that the United States could have won the war. Based on her vastly superior resources, Britain should have gained a quick and easy victory. A brief comparison of Britain's resources, and those of America shows how much inferior the Americans were in almost every respect.

There was, first, the matter of money to finance the war. Britain had plenty of "hard money"—gold and silver coinage to pay troops and provide guns, ammunition, equipment, supplies of food and ships. America, on the other hand, had so little money that the fighting men often went unpaid and shortages of arms and supplies were common all through the Revolution.

The problem for the Americans in raising money was that the only sort of American central government, the Continental Congress, did not have the power to levy taxes on the colonies to carry on the war. It was up to

The value of paper money, like this six-dollar bill, issued by the Continental Congress during the Revolution, soon became far less than the amount printed on the bills.

each colony to do what it could, or would, to pay the cost of the Revolution. Consequently, the Continental Congress was forced to print paper money, and since these paper bills were not backed by gold or silver they soon became almost worthless. "Not worth a Continental" (the name by which these paper bills were called) became an expression to describe anything of little or no value.

As for military and naval fighting men, Britain could and did send vast numbers of troops and seamen to wage the war against America. There was seldom difficulty in landing troops, since throughout practically the entire war the British held important seaports in the colonies, first Boston, then New York, as well as Quebec in Canada. At various times they also controlled other major seaports such as Philadelphia, Charleston and Savannah. Thus the British were able to make massive landings of armies, and their powerful fleets discouraged any attempt by America's meager sea power to drive off invaders, up until the final years of the war, when French naval power came to the aid of the Americans.

In fighting ability, Britain's soldiers had every advantage in training, discipline and war experience. The German Hessians, Brunswickers and Waldeckers hired to fight in the Revolution for Britain were professional soldiers whose business was war. The only time they failed George III of Britain and their own German masters who profited from these mercenaries' efforts was at Trenton on the morning after Christmas, 1776.

America's troops, at least in the early years of the war, were mostly untrained, undisciplined and disorganized. Therefore, the defeat of the British expedition at Concord, the battle at Bunker Hill and the American success at driving the enemy out of Boston seem unbelievable.

Later on, in the major battles of the Revolution, it is equally fantastic that the Americans were able to win so many important victories. Able trainers of fighting men like de Kalb and Kosciuszko, who came to America from abroad, were able to aid the American generals in welding the raw recruits into the Continental soldiers who were the mainstay of the American armies. But in almost every important battle the American leaders had to contend with the problem of large groups of undependable militia who would run for their lives before British musket volleys and cannon fire.

In spite of Britain's overall potential superiority, the Americans did have a few advantages. In some engagements with the British their style of fighting gave them an edge. The British and German armies were trained in the

European type of warfare. They fought by certain rules which the Americans sometimes were able to disregard and thus prevail over their enemies. An example is the bloody near-massacre during the British retreat from Concord when the Minute Men, swarming in from surrounding villages, took cover behind trees, bushes, stone walls, houses and barns to pick off the redcoats, whose march, at the start, was in perfect military formation. This method was used to advantage by the Americans in some other engagements, notably in the South.

One other minor advantage was the marksmanship of some American units equipped with the famous long rifles, especially Daniel Morgan's Virginians. On the other hand, the British and German armies were far better equipped with weapons, particularly in the early years of the war when the usual type of muskets used by the Americans were largely old, inefficient ones.

Also, in the most important battles of the Revolution, American wilderness-type of fighting could rarely be used and the opposing armies fought in a way that was closer to the European style. On the whole, the advantage in most respects lay with the British and Germans, at least until French aid to America became substantial in the latter part of the war.

Considering the leaders on each side, with perhaps one exception Britain's generals in America should have outshone the American commanders. All the British leaders had good records as professional officers who were well versed in strategy and tactics. Gage was the only high-ranking British general in America whose abilities during the Revolution did not measure up in that respect.

Of America's generals, George Washington, Nathanael Greene, Benedict Arnold, Daniel Morgan and John Stark (Stark's glory rests on a single battle) matched the skill of the British generals, but only because of the blunders committed by the enemy commanders and the bungling of the government leaders in Britain, including George III. Save for the numerous glaring mistakes in judgment and strategy made by the British, the names of the American leaders would probably be pretty well forgotten today, even that of Benedict Arnold, since the American rebels should have been forced to their knees long before the time when Arnold committed treason. It is true that American commanders, particularly Washington and Greene, made grave mistakes and that the Continental Congress made even more serious ones, but the errors of the British generals and the government in London were worse.

All these factors which have only been briefly outlined here show why America won a war it should have lost. In the siege of Boston alone, the British, by striking quickly and efficiently, should have ended a rebellion that as yet could scarcely be called a war. During the campaigns in New York and New Jersey the British had every chance to win total victory. And so it went as time passed, until France came to America's aid and the American Revolution, which should long have been over, continued on to gain freedom for Britain's American colonies.

2

Not-So-Mighty Ticonderoga

ON MAY 25, 1775, THE FRIGATE "CERBERUS" OF HIS BRITISH Majesty's Navy arrived in Boston. She carried three distinguished passengers—Maj. Gens. William Howe, Henry Clinton and John Burgoyne. They were to help Gen. Thomas Gage, commander in chief of the British armies in America, crush the American rebellion that had begun at Lexington and Concord on April 19.

Since in mythology Cerberus was a three-headed dog, a wit in Boston wrote a rhyme that spread quickly and gave the American patriots in and around Boston a good laugh:

> *Behold the* Cerberus *the Atlantic plough,*
> *Her precious cargo, Burgoyne, Clinton, Howe.*
> *Bow, wow, wow!*

Standing on the *Cerberus'* foredeck, John Burgoyne, in all the pomp and magnificence of his general's scarlet, white and gold uniform, let his gaze wander over the town lying before him. He was a handsome man, debonair, with a devil-may-care look, and as faultlessly dressed as any London man of fashion.

Knowing that Boston was under siege by the American patriots, he asked how many there were of them.

"Boston is surrounded on the land side by ten thousand country people, sir," an aide replied.

"And how many British regulars are in the town?"

"About five thousand, General."

"What!" cried Burgoyne. "Ten thousand peasants keep five thousand King's troops shut up! Well, let *us* get in and we'll soon find elbow room."

Burgoyne was to live to regret those words, as well as his later remark that the Americans were a "rabble in arms." Yet there was no reason to expect that the British would not be able to subdue quickly all the rebellious American colonies.

It took the Americans over six years to win it, but time after time during those years British generals had a chance either to rout or destroy an American army and follow up the victory with a surrender. What is amazing is that the British generals and their government in London could

Dashing "Gentleman Johnny" Burgoyne was contemptuous of the American Revolutionary army at first, but not when he was forced to surrender to them at Saratoga.
NEW YORK PUBLIC LIBRARY PICTURE COLLECTION

have been so slow moving and incompetent as to throw away so many chances.

Yet despite the indications of an easy British victory, troubles for the redcoats began at Fort Ticonderoga in May, 1775. Lake Champlain, nearly two hundred miles long, was an obvious route for a British invasion from Canada. Twice, powerful British expeditions were sent to gain control of Lake Champlain, the Hudson River and the territory between the two, and thus isolate New England, the most rebellious of the thirteen American colonies. This plan was often referred to as "cutting the head off the Revolution."

Ticonderoga was the key to the whole operation. Lake Champlain, broad at its northern end, gradually narrows until it peters out to a snakelike wispy tail near Whitehall, New York, which in 1775 was called Skenesboro.

About twenty-five miles north of Skenesboro, on the New York side of the lake, stood Fort Ticonderoga. It guarded an especially narrow strait about a quarter of a mile wide between the New York colony and the New Hampshire Grants, which today comprise Vermont. Ever since the British had captured Fort Ticonderoga from the French in 1759, toward the end of the French and Indian War, the fortress had flown the Union Jack.

Since the lake was surrounded by wilderness with no through road on either side, an army from Canada must hold Ticonderoga in order to get soldiers, heavy cannon and other military equipment and supplies south of the lake. Otherwise, the fort's cannon could blow an enemy fleet out of the water at short range.

Although the British knew the strategic importance of Fort Ticonderoga, throughout 1774 and the early months of 1775, when the American Revolution was rumbling like a volcano getting ready to blow its top, the British did nothing to make sure Ticonderoga was held. In the more than fifteen years since the French had surrendered it, the fortress itself and its many strong defense outposts had been crumbling, and were in need of major repairs.

There was a British garrison of sorts at Ticonderoga, commanded by Capt. William Delaplace. The garrison included one other officer, Lieut. Jocelyn Feltman, and two artillerymen, two sergeants and forty-four privates, half of whom were elderly and decrepit.

During the summer of 1774, when the British government should have been sensitive to a potential American revolution, a strong, well-equipped reinforcement could have been sent from Canada to mend Ticonderoga's defenses and be ready to hold this bulwark that controlled the water highway from Canada south. If this precaution had been taken the British should have been able to hold the fortress if the Americans attacked it.

This British neglect enabled an American patriot to carry out a daring plan. In the New Hampshire Grants to which both New York and New Hampshire claimed ownership lived a giant braggart of a settler with a thunderous voice and a vast store of audacious brass in his character. Ethan Allen's speech was laced with oaths sizzling enough to make the leaves on the trees curl up and fall off. Ethan fancied himself a great leader, but the truth was that his military career before 1775, while exciting, was not impressive.

The New York authorities sent sheriffs with posses to the New Hampshire Grants, armed with writs of ejectment to drive out the settlers who had bought their land from New Hampshire, so that New York settlers could move in. Ethan rounded up a band of tough, red-necked, hard-drinking, brawling farmers he called his Green Mountain Boys.

For some years Ethan Allen and his famous band fought a "war" with the "Yorkers." It was not really a war, and no one was killed, but when Ethan and his men caught an encroaching Yorker they either whipped him with what they called the "beech seal" or the "twigs of the wilderness," or frightened the wits out of him with such dire threats that many prospective Yorker settlers fled for their lives. Then came the Revolution, and although many settlers of the Grants thought he was crazy, Ethan Allen decided to lead the Green Mountain Boys across Lake Champlain and capture mighty Fort Ticonderoga. Just as the Green Mountain Boys were about to march for the fort from the settlement of Castleton, a small delegation of volunteers from Connecticut appeared, also bound for Ticonderoga. They were led by Benedict Arnold, who was to become America's most infamous traitor. At Castleton he announced haughtily that *he*, not Ethan Allen, was in command of the expedition against "Ti."

These two formidable adversaries faced each other in the taproom of Zadock Remington's tavern in Castleton. There was a ferocious argument but Ethan kept the command, although an enraged Arnold, kept close beside him on the march.

What with additional Green Mountain Boys rounded up on the way, about two hundred men gathered that night at Hand's Cove across from Ticonderoga. To Ethan's dismay, a detachment he had sent to Skenesboro to seize some boats he knew were there had not arrived.

Undaunted, Allen sent men out to pick up whatever boats could be found along the shore. The expedition yielded only a few canoes and one scow. Then miraculously, another scow appeared. The stories of how it was obtained vary, but the best one, if true, concerns two young boys who overheard one of Allen's searchers asking a lakeside settler about boats.

They knew of a big scow belonging to Col. Philip Skene, a rich Tory who owned everything in Skenesboro and lived in a magnificent manor there. The boys got hold of muskets, powder horns, a jug of rum and bullet pouches, probably without the knowledge of the owners, their fathers. A black man, Captain Jack, who was extremely fond of rum, was in charge of Skene's scow. The boys bribed him with the jug to take them in the scow to Hand's Cove where, they said, they were going on a "wolf hunt." Upon landing, Allen's men seized the scow.

Although Allen's flotilla could carry only about eighty men, it was near dawn, and since his best chance was to strike by surprise before daylight, he set out with eighty-three of his force.

All was quiet as darkness turned to gray in the east on the morning of May 10, 1775, and the invaders landed. A half-dozing British sentry at a wicket gate in the walls of the fort suddenly saw a gigantic figure that looked as big as a modern tank bearing down on him. He managed to pull the trigger of his musket; it misfired and he took to his heels, yelling like a madman.

Exactly what happened after that is a maze of different accounts. It is aggravating, in reading Allen's own *Narrative*, to find that this windy man wrote few details of it, devoting most of the book to the story of his sufferings a little later as a prisoner of the British. However, Allen, with Arnold close at hand and followed by the Green Mountain Boys, reached the inner parade of the fort. There Allen roared, "Fall in, all of you!" But the Green Mountain Boys ignored the order and scattered in all directions toward the barracks surrounding the open space.

Ethan Allen demands the surrender of Ticonderoga "in the name of the great Jehovah and the Continental Congress."

A redcoat with bayonet fixed came hurtling out of the barracks and lunged at a Green Mountain Boy. Allen leaped between them and felled the Britisher with a tremendous blow, using the flat of his huge sword. He then ordered the fallen man to take him to the fort's commander. The fellow staggered to his feet and reeled up an outside stairway leading to Captain Delaplace's quarters, followed closely by Ethan.

Again the accounts differ. One says that Allen, hammering on the commander's door, yelled, "Come out, you, old skunk, or we'll slaughter your garrison!"

Captain Delaplace appeared, blinking sleepily, partly dressed but carrying his trousers.

"Surrender this fort instantly!" Allen thundered.

"By what authority?" the captain quavered.

Allen himself, in the *Narrative*, has given his famous reply: "In the name of the great Jehovah and the Continental Congress!" Why he brought God into it is unknown, but Ethan professed to be a religious man, a member of the sect called Deists, knew his Bible thoroughly and often quoted from it, twisting the words to suit his own purposes in a way that scandalized the minister of the church in Bennington.

Delaplace had no choice but to hand Allen his sword. The British garrison then threw down their arms, and the Green Mountain Boys, having discovered the fort's stock of rum, celebrated joyously and drunkenly. Allen described it in the pompous language of which he was fond: "The sun seemed to rise that morning with a supreme luster; and Ticonderoga and its dependencies smiled on its conquerors, who tossed about the flowing bowl and wished success to Congress and the liberty and freedom of America."

If Ticonderoga had been repaired and strongly garrisoned, Ethan Allen would have had no chance to capture it. Captain Delaplace had long suspected an attack was coming. On September 1, 1774, he wrote the British commander in chief, Gage, in Boston, saying Ticonderoga was in terrible condition. But as usual there was a maze of official government red tape to be gotten through before the fort could be restored. Gage referred the request to Lord William Dartmouth, Secretary of State for the Colonies in London. By the time he got permission to put Ticonderoga in shape it was mid-winter, and all routes to the fort were virtually impassable.

When the spring of 1775 came, Gage wrote Carleton in Canada to send a regiment to Ticonderoga. Before it could get there, Ethan Allen had leaped like a tiger from the wilderness.

Ethan Allan had won with little difficulty a victory that was to make him famous, though his later military career was most inglorious. Ticonderoga's capture not only heartened the patriots of the American colonies, but it spoiled a British invasion later on.

In the early fall of 1776 Britain tried to recapture Fort Ticonderoga when Gen. Sir Guy Carleton, with 13,000 men and an enormous fleet came up Lake Champlain from Canada. Benedict Arnold, who could play the admiral as brilliantly as the general, fought the British armada almost to a standstill, but in the end he was overwhelmed and his crude little fleet, built mostly on the lake, was nearly destroyed. Yet the battle delayed Carleton's arrival

The fortress of Ticonderoga, restored today as it looked during
the Revolution. COURTESY, FORT TICONDEROGA MUSEUM

at Ticonderoga until late October.

If the fortress had been in British hands he could have
wintered there and gone on in the spring. But fearing he
might not retake Ticonderoga, though he should easily
have been able to, and facing the onset of winter two
hundred miles from his base of supplies, he turned back
rather than risk besieging the fort.

There was one other highly important result of Allen's
victory at Ticonderoga. But for the fortress' capture the
American army's siege of Boston would almost certainly
have failed.

3

The Rabble in Arms

IF GENERAL GAGE HAD STRUCK SWIFTLY AND WITH A STRONG force soon after the American Revolution began at Lexington and Concord, he probably could have destroyed, captured or sent the Americans besieging Boston into disorderly flight. Until well after Gen. George Washington took command of what then became known as the Continental army in Cambridge on July 3, 1775, Burgoyne was right when he spoke of the Americans as a "rabble in arms."

It would be unfair to call all the American soldiers riffraff. There were many brave, dedicated men among them who obeyed orders, were excellent fighters, expert marksmen and all-around good soldiers. The high-ranking officers were mostly good men, as well as some of those of lower rank.

Unfortunately, there were also many of the soldiers who were of the lowest sort. They obeyed orders when they felt like it, went home for short or long visits when they felt like it, deserted, were drunk much of the time, robbed their companions, lived in filth and made no attempt to improve their quarters, which no one can deny were poor. The American camps ringing the land surrounding Boston were not a pretty sight. Many diaries and journals kept by American Revolutionary soldiers are still in existence or printed in historical records. Some give revealing glimpses of what the camps outside Boston were like.

Some of them record punishments:

"Man whipped 20 lashes for striking his officer."

"A man whipped for stealing."

"Man given 20 stripes [lashes] and [fined] 30 shillings for stealing."

"One man was whipped and drummed out for stealing. He was a bold and unshamefaced wretch."

"Man found guilty of choking and cursing, fined 1 shilling and to confess to the man that he choked."

Insubordination was usually dealt with sternly:

"Man set in the pillory for writing an infamous letter about Col. Brewer."

"This day there was a man drummed out of camp for saying the general was a damned Tory."

"Bennony Robins put under guard [for] talking sassy to our captain."

"William Gale tried by court-martial for defaming the adjutant; sentenced to make confession at the head of the regiment and be discharged from the army."

"Man whipped 20 lashes for striking his officer."

Yet there were untrained officers who stood for insubordination. An observer overheard a captain in the camp at Roxbury say to a private: "Bill, go and bring a pail of water for the mess." The private replied, "I shan't; it is your turn now, captain, I got the last."

Many journal entries describe desertions:

"A Regular of the 5th Regiment deserted . . . he was standing sentry with another Regular, he took the flint out of his own gun, hove out the priming and spit in the pan [which held the small charge of priming powder that, when ignited by sparks as the musket's hammer struck the flint, set off the main powder charge inside the gun], then offered to swap with his partner and give him a drink in the morning, until he accepted . . . made his escape, his partner snapped his gun to no purpose. . . ."

"This morning one of our riflemen received 39 lashes for desertion and stealing a $20 bill . . . he was drummed out of camp to 52 drummers and 52 whiffers [fifers]."

An historian, describing the behavior of soldiers in the army besieging Boston, said, ". . . they might stay for a spell to see what was going on in camp, or they might plead the state of their farms . . . as a reason—not an excuse—for going home."

Maj. Gen. Artemas Ward was the nearest thing to a commander in chief of the army. Before Washington arrived, Ward was in command of the Massachusetts troops and usually those from the other colonies. He wrote the Massachusetts Provincial Congress about the desertion problem: "My situation is such that if I have no enlisting orders immediately I shall be left all alone. It is impossible to keep the men here unless something is done. . . ."

As for drinking among the soldiers, a comment in a Revolutionary soldier's journal written in his camp in

February, 1776, gives some rather astonishing evidence:

"This morning we went to rollcall and there was a man killed himself a-drinking jen [gin]. There was two men drunk 44 glasses, one lived. . . ."

Living conditions in the camp were enough to drive a man to drink. During the early part of the siege there were few tents for the men, though eventually some more were made from sailcloth. Most soldiers made huts of boards from houses ruined by British cannon fire; others used stone, turf and bricks.

Many of the people living in the area around Boston had abandoned their homes. The houses which were still livable were eagerly seized by the troops. The trouble was that so many men crowded into them that they were as bad if not worse than the huts. In Cambridge, Harvard College was taken over for the use of the army, but again, too many crowded into the buildings.

During the winter of 1775–76 it was reported that they were "so closely stored in the Colleges they were lousy." And there was a serious shortage of blankets and uniforms. A description of the typical soldier in the besieging army says he was "a grimy figure, his head wrapped in an old bandanna, a short pipe between his teeth, stripped of his upper garments, his lower limbs encased in leather breeches, yarn stockings and hobnail shoes."

Feeding the army was another problem. Each town was supposed to send food for its own troops, but the plan was badly organized and supplies only dribbled in. Two days after the Revolution began, all eatables that could be spared were collected in Cambridge, and Harvard was a source of kitchen and table utensils. A shipment of beef and pork bound for the British in Boston was seized, as well as a large supply of ship's biscuit supposed to be destined for the British squadron in Boston harbor.

Cattle and hay were captured under the noses of the British in several raids on islands in the harbor. The American army's commissary general was ordered to supply the troops with provisions "in the best manner he can, without spending time on exactness." In other words, he was to seize whatever he could lay his hands on without being particular as to where it came from. He managed to furnish enough food to allow the soldiers to live on scanty rations, which, no doubt, depleted the food supply of many residents of the countryside.

Arms and ammunition were scarce, even though most of the volunteers who flocked into headquarters in Cambridge brought their own muskets. In mid-June, the American army was short a thousand small arms. There were almost no bayonets, only a few large, ancient cannon, a handful of mortars and howitzers, and sixteen field guns, most of them unusable.

This was the state of the American army early in the summer of 1775. While more men poured in, it was still a poor apology for an army, even after General Washington took command and had begun turning disorder into order and welding a fighting army out of the rabble.

Meanwhile, the British army, cooped up in Boston, had what the Americans lacked—trained, disciplined fighting men equipped with muskets, pistols, bayonets, plenty of ammunition and heavy cannon, especially the big guns of the large naval squadron lying in Boston harbor, which included four powerful ships-of-the-line, each carrying at least sixty cannon.

The British had suffered a humiliating defeat on the expedition to Concord April 19. But it was not at Lexington, where the Minute Men on the green had been thrown into terrified retreat by the volley fired by Maj. John Pitcairn's redcoats, nor at Concord Bridge, where a detachment of a couple of hundred British troops, outnumbered perhaps two to one by Minute Men, were repulsed in a skirmish. It was during the homeward march of the entire British expedition to Boston, with Minute Men swarming in from all over the surrounding countryside, that what had begun as an orderly march turned into a bloody rout, with many redcoats killed and wounded and the rest saved only by British reinforcements sent out from Boston.

The American victory was far more than what the Brit-

The Americans on the green at Lexington were no match for Maj. Pitcairn's detachment of redcoats when the first shots of the revolution were fired April 19, 1775.

ish tried to pass off as a skirmish. But immediately after
the battle the British had the overwhelming power to
crush the American besiegers of Boston, whose defenses
encircled the land end of the peninsula on which the city
then stood. The redcoats, tired of living on short rations
and thoroughly bored with doing nothing but sentry duty
and other daily routine, were ready for a showdown.

On June 17 Gage sent his senior major general, Howe,
across the Charles River with about 1,500 troops to assault
and capture Breed's and Bunker's hills above Charlestown. He could scarcely have made a worse military judgment, but he was forced into it by his own slothfulness.
He and the other three generals were enjoying themselves
in Boston. Rich Tories, with plenty of "hard money"—
silver and gold, not the almost worthless paper money the
Continental Congress in Philadelphia was printing—were
able to pay for luxuries smuggled in by greedy profiteers
on the shore outside Boston. These Tories were delighted
to entertain the generals, especially the dashing, elegant
Burgoyne. There were balls and plays, including a drama
written by Burgoyne, who was an accomplished playwright.

While the generals were wining, dining and dancing,
the Americans stole a march on them and fortified Breed's
Hill in the night. There was no easy way for the British to
get at the Americans except by a charge up the steep hill.
The warships anchored in the Charles River could not
elevate their guns enough to bombard the American
defenses.

Howe's redcoats charged up the hill into a deadly hail
of American bullets. Breed's Hill was taken, but only after
two bloody charges had been repelled and the British had

The British victory at Bunker Hill in 1775 was one of the most
disastrous for them of the entire Revolution.

suffered such frightful casualties that an English wit
remarked, "We are certainly victorious, but if we
have eight more such victories there will be nobody left to
bring news of them."

Having gained control of Breed's Hill, the British
mounted cannon on Bunker's Hill in back of it, which was
higher and therefore better for bombarding the American
defenses. This battle actually took place almost entirely
on Breed's Hill, and would more accurately be called by
that name.

After the heavy British losses, Gage was recalled to
England in disgrace and Howe took command. Howe was
a dark complexioned, rather coarse looking, easygoing
man who drank too much, gambled too much and was a
devil with the ladies. He was also too busy to see that his
best opportunity to crush the Revolution was in striking
quickly, but not, as he had so stubbornly done, in charging
time after time up a steep hill.

Boston, except for the British troops, the Tories and the few patriots who had not left the town before Gage had put a stop to such departures, was now like a tomb. The busy clatter of its many shipyards, the creak of windlasses and rumble of drays on the wharves were stilled, and idle ships rotted at their moorings. On the streets that had bustled with the activity of sea trade, grass grew a foot tall between the cobblestone paving. The British troops, still hungry and bored, got into mischief and often mistreated patriots who had not left the city. These conditions should have prompted Howe to action.

In October, again too late, the British government sent transports loaded with oxen, sheep, hogs, beer, coal, wood, food for the horses and almost five hundred thousand pounds sterling in hard money. Winter storms delayed the vessels, more than half the animals aboard died, the vegetables in their cargoes rotted, gales drove many transports ashore on the American coast or far to the southward to seek shelter in the West Indies. Only a few ships ever reached Boston, though they did, along with ships from Nova Scotia and the West Indies, bring some relief to feed the redcoats.

Yet during the spring or early summer of 1775, all Howe had to do was to sail about a mile and a half from Boston across to Dorchester Heights with a strong force protected by his warships' big guns and mount cannon there. Dorchester Heights, like Boston, was on a peninsula at the eastern end of the American chain of defenses surrounding the land side of Boston. The Americans had been working at top speed to complete their defenses, but Dorchester Heights was one of their weaker defenses because they lacked cannon to mount on the hill. It would have been a key point for the British from which to bombard that end of the American lines and to launch a powerful attack on the whole disorganized American army.

Even after Washington had taken command and the Continental army was being trained and disciplined, Howe could have struck. On December 31, 1775, the enlistments of the entire army would expire and the men would go home. January 1 came and many hundreds of soldiers left. But a number of colonies responded to Washington's appeals, and he was able to build up a new force of about 10,000 recruits and militia. But if Howe had struck at the year end's crucial moment, his redcoats

Gen. Burgoyne called the ragged American army a "rabble in arms," but Gen. George Washington started it on the way to victory when he took command at Cambridge on July 3, 1775.

British Gen. Sir William Howe's rather
inglorious Revolutionary career began
in Boston, but the Americans chased
him out in 1776.

would have had an easy and devastating victory. It is hard
to believe that his spies did not inform him of the American weakness at that time.

The Americans, meanwhile, were fully aware that their
defenses had an Achilles' heel—one fatal weak spot. They
had still been unable to fortify Dorchester Heights for lack
of cannon.

But a tubby young man in the army, Henry Knox, who
had been a bookseller in Boston and whose only
knowledge of weapons came from books he had devoured
in his own shop, had an idea. Why not send an expedition
to Ticonderoga? There were plenty of big cannon there
that could be brought to Cambridge and used to fortify
Dorchester Heights.

Washington made Knox a colonel and chief of ordnance
for the Continental army—and sent him to Ticonderoga.
He and a force of tough woodsmen left Cambridge in mid-
November and reached Ticonderoga December 5, 1775.
In the bitter weeks that followed, Knox and his men overcame almost insuperable difficulties in hauling the cannon
on ox sleds to Albany, crossing the Hudson River and then

pushing through the wilderness and deep snow over the Berkshire Hills to the Continental army's camp.

At long last Howe had decided to strike at Dorchester Heights. But when he awoke on the morning of March 5, 1776, he found that the hill had been fortified in secrecy during the night by the Americans with Ticonderoga's cannon. Nevertheless, the obstinate Howe was determined to attack anyway. According to an eighteenth-century British historian, one of the redcoats in the expedition was heard to say to another: "It will be another Bunker's Hill affair or worse."

It might have been if Howe's staff officers had not strongly counseled him against the assault five hours before it was to take place. This time the general listened to reason and decided to evacuate Boston. The British army sailed away on March 17.

Thus the Americans won a victory without a fight simply because Howe waited too long. And this was also the second important result of the British incompetence that had permitted Ethan Allen's capture of Ticonderoga. Without its guns mounted on Dorchester Heights, Washington's army, strengthened though it had been, was in no shape to defeat the full force of British might in Boston.

4

Charleston, 1776, a Hornets' Nest

MOST OF GENERAL HOWE'S ARMY, WHEN IT SAILED FROM Boston, went to Halifax, Nova Scotia, where they camped before making their next attack against the Americans. A few companies, however, under General Clinton, sailed for New York in a transport, escorted by the 20-gun frigate *Mercury*, and anchored in the lower harbor there.

But New York was only the first stop. A big British armada was already on its way across the Atlantic to rendezvous with Clinton's ships off the coast of the Carolinas. The armada was under command of Adm. Sir Peter Parker, and included his flagship, the big, 50-gun *Bristol*, one other 50-gun warship, four 28-gun frigates and one of 20 guns, an 8-gun sloop, a 6-gun schooner and a bomb ketch mounting six guns and two mortars. Escorted by this naval might were more than thirty transports carrying about 2,500 troops commanded by Lord Charles Cornwallis. Once the two forces were united, the command would be Clinton's.

The naval squadron was impressive, and while the number of troops was comparatively small, Clinton believed the expedition was strong enough to accomplish its purpose, which he stated was not to capture the southern colonies but to reinforce the Loyalist inhabitants against the patriots. Josiah Martin, who had been royal governor of South Carolina until patriots forced him to flee to the protection of a British warship, suggested that once the many Tories in North Carolina were well armed they could easily regain control of royal government there, protected by Tory troops who were American natives of the colony.

Yet Clinton had received different advice from William Tryon in New York. Tryon had been royal governor of North Carolina until American patriots drove him out when he levied crushing taxes on the inhabitants to build himself a palatial mansion. He fled North Carolina when an organization called the Regulators rose in a bloody rebellion against him. With this uprising in mind, Tryon told Clinton he would have no easy time in establishing British law and order in North Carolina.

Gen. Sir Henry Clinton attacked Charleston, South Carolina in 1776 with a powerful British armada of warships and a good-sized force of soldiers, but was given a terrible beating by the Americans.

When Clinton's two ships and Sir Peter Parker's fleet met off Cape Fear on the North Carolina coast, former Governor Martin admitted that the patriots were in control of the colony as far as a hundred miles inland. Clinton also learned that in February 2,000 American militia had routed a Tory force of the same size in North Carolina. He decided it would be better to strike at Charleston, South Carolina, the most important seaport of the southern colonies.

It appeared certain that even though Clinton had only a small number of troops, with his strong naval power he could capture the city, especially since there were no Continental troops to defend it. The British general did not know that an American privateer had captured a British vessel in Chesapeake Bay carrying mails, which included a letter from Lord George Germain, Secretary of State for the Colonies, to the royal governor of Maryland, Robert Eden, telling about the expedition which would go "in the first place to North Carolina and from thence either to South Carolina or Virginia. . . ."

As a result, American Maj. Gen. Charles Lee was ordered south. On the way he picked up 1,000 Virginia and South Carolina Continentals.

Sir Peter Parker's armada was late in arriving at the rendezvous off Cape Fear because a violent storm had scattered his vessels. It was May 30, 1776, before the combined expedition sailed for Charleston. Although General Lee learned the British squadron had left the rendezvous, he did not know in which direction it would go, but he decided Charleston was the most logical place. He had no sooner arrived there than Sir Peter's fleet anchored off the harbor.

Navigating into Charleston harbor was difficult, for several sandbars left only narrow entrances through which seagoing naval vessels could steer. The harbor was also protected by Fort Johnson on its west side and Fort Sullivan on the east.

Fort Johnson, on Jones Island, was well armed with twenty big 18- and 25-pounder cannon, and at another location on the same island but nearer Charleston was a battery of twelve heavy cannon. Fort Sullivan was only half completed. It was planned as a square redoubt with a long, pointed bastion extending out from each corner. But at the time only the south and east walls were finished, leaving the other two sides open. Each wall was composed of two parallel walls of palmetto logs, fastened together at intervals by crosspieces. The palisades were sixteen feet apart, the space between them filled with sand.

General Lee thought the unfinished Fort Sullivan was indefensible, but both John Rutledge, elected governor of South Carolina by the patriots, and Col. William Moultrie insisted it could withstand any kind of naval gunfire, and finally General Lee dropped his objections. Impossible as it seems, Rutledge and Moultrie were right.

Until the British admiral could mark the entrance channel with buoys he could not leave his deepwater anchorage. Clinton looked the situation over and decided not to wait, but go ahead with 500 troops to probe out an attack route to Fort Sullivan.

He landed them on Long Island, whose western end was separated from Sullivan's Island only by a narrow strait called The Breach. In most places it was only about a foot and a half deep, and when Clinton tried to bring his men over in boats they grounded in the sand. They tried

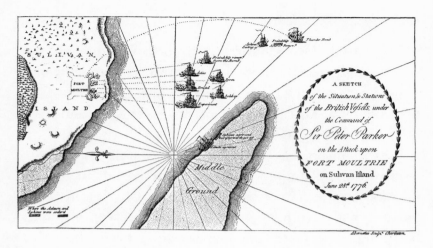

The position of the British squadron when it tried in vain to smash Fort Sullivan (later renamed Moultrie) and met with a crushing defeat. NEW YORK PUBLIC LIBRARY PICTURE COLLECTION

wading, but found The Breach was full of treacherous holes, many seven feet deep.

So Clinton's men, numbering 2,500 in all, and a detachment of Americans just opposite on Sullivan's Island peppered each other throughout the battle with fire that did no great harm, since both sides were protected by defenses they threw up.

It was going to be up to Admiral Parker to run his warships past the forts to the inner harbor and bombard Charleston into submission. But he had still another problem—his two great 50-gun warships were of too deep draft to pass over a sandbar at the harbor entrance. To lighten the ships he had to dismount their cannon, land them, sail his vessels over the bar and then remount the guns, which took him two weeks.

Early on the morning of June 28 the fleet moved into the channel intending to blast unfinished Fort Sullivan to pieces and then sail on into the harbor unmolested. There were two lines of warships. One, including the vessels with the largest and most numerous guns, dropped anchor within about two hundred yards of the fort, at very close range. These ships then swung about so they could fire broadsides directly into the fort. In the second line, a few hundred yards farther offshore, were three 28-gun frigates. Nearby, protected by another frigate, was the bomb ketch *Thunder*.

The line closest to the fort, with eight warships, began to slam a terrific weight of metal into Fort Sullivan. The

Unfinished Fort Sullivan's walls were weak, but of unusual construction that allowed the British warships' cannon balls to bury themselves harmlessly in sand.

intensity of the fire is shown by the number of rounds fired by the British that day—reported to be ten thousand; at least seven thousand balls were later found on Sullivan's Island.

Such a pounding should have reduced Fort Sullivan to kindling. But Governor Rutledge and Colonel Moultrie knew what they were doing when they insisted that the fort could withstand the heaviest kind of fire. If it had been built of hardwood it would soon have been smashed to rubble, but palmetto is very soft, almost spongy wood. The British cannonballs simply passed through the outer palisade as if it had been so much butter and then buried themselves harmlessly in the sand between the parallel rows of palisades.

As for the Americans inside the fort, they replied slowly and coolly to the British fire. They were short of ammunition and tried to make every shot count. The American gunners concentrated their fire on the two 50-gun ships. They shot away the flagship *Bristol*'s bow anchor cable, and she swung with the tide, exposing her quarterdeck to direct fire from ashore. Every gun in the fort was then turned to rake her fore and aft. They blasted the mainmast to pieces and damaged the mizzenmast so badly that it had to be cut down. Before the *Bristol* could be swung back into position every officer aboard her was either killed or wounded and for a time Admiral Parker, himself slightly wounded, was the only officer on the quarterdeck.

When an hour's fierce bombardment failed to demolish Fort Sullivan, the three frigates in the outer line began to move toward the inner harbor. Their plan was to get around to the eastern side of the fort. There their cannon could rake the fort's gun platforms and put them out of action.

Unfortunately, having seen what terrible punishment the inside line of warships was taking, this second line made too wide a sweep to keep out of range. In the middle of the harbor mouth was a large sandbar, the Middle Ground, on which all three frigates ran aground. Whether Sir Peter Parker's captains had been warned or knew of the Middle Ground, the records do not show. But the chief responsibility fell upon Sir Peter Parker's shoulders. He and Clinton did not get along well, anyhow, and since the accident resulted in the loss of the battle of Charleston, bitter accusations afterward flew between the admiral and the general.

Of the three grounded frigates, two, the *Acteon* and *Sphinx*, collided with considerable damage in their frantic efforts to get free of the bar. That afternoon the *Sphinx* and the third warship, the *Syren*, did get off by kedging— carrying out anchors to a distance in small boats and then hauling in on the anchor cables. Once free they limped back out of the harbor to make repairs. But the *Acteon* remained stuck fast in the sand and was finally set afire and burned by her crew.

Thus the battle of Charleston was decided. Clinton made one more attempt to cross The Breach, but the Americans easily repulsed him. That night the badly-damaged British warships withdrew outside the harbor to make repairs. They had suffered a fearful hammering from the American guns.

The official British report shows 64 men killed and 131 wounded, with 111 of the casualties aboard the *Bristol*.

However, British losses may have been even higher. A British army surgeon, treating the wounded aboard the *Bristol*, wrote in his diary that aboard the flagship alone over 300 men had been lost. American losses, on the other hand, were very light. Twelve men were killed, 5 more died later of their wounds, and 20 others were wounded.

During the Revolution the British lost many chances to defeat the Americans, and the Charleston expedition is a good example of the ineptitude of the British army and navy. Clinton listened to bad advice and was not familiar enough with the approaches to the city. Furthermore, Charleston could almost surely have been taken if Admiral Parker's fleet had gotten within bombardment range, but that chance was thrown away when the three frigates which could have destroyed Fort Sullivan went aground, due to ignorance of the Middle Ground's location or bad handling of the ships.

Thus this first try at subduing the southern colonies cost the British dearly in money, loss of men and time. It was a fiasco that, even if successful, could not have conquered all the southern colonies. The British could have used their efforts better elsewhere.

5

Howe Wins and Loses on Long Island

AT THIS POINT IN THE WAR, THE BRITISH GOVERNMENT WAS finally beginning to realize that a few regiments of redcoats were not going to be able to subdue the American colonies, and that some of the great military power that Britain had in abundance would have to be employed. When General Howe was ready for his next campaign he had an immense army supported by a powerful naval fleet. No military expert would have given General Washington's Continental army on Manhattan Island a chance to repel a British assault on New York City.

General Howe had sailed from Boston with his troops to Halifax on March 27, 1776. On June 25 he arrived in lower New York Bay with 7,000 soldiers in three warships. By this time Washington, who had moved from Boston to New York, had assembled about 19,000 men. Although this was too large an army for Howe's troops to overwhelm, the Americans were mostly raw recruits, untrained and poorly equipped. But for the British, Howe's 7,000 were only a small beginning.

Four days after Howe reached New York Bay, 45 more

British ships came in, followed the next day by 82 more. The transports of the two fleets landed 9,300 redcoats on Staten Island, where Howe had established his headquarters. On July 12, 150 more ships anchored in the bay, commanded by Howe's brother, Admiral Lord Richard Howe, whose complexion, like the general's, was so dark that his sailors called him "Black Dick."

Still more warships and transports arrived. Adm. Sir Peter Parker came in with nine fighting vessels and thirty transports carrying General Clinton and the 2,500 men who had survived the attempt to take Charleston. These British troops, badly beaten at Charleston, cheered up when they saw the military strength the Howes had assembled to assault New York City. This great host of power was increased even more on August 12, when six men-of-war and twenty-eight transports landed 2,600 more British troops and 8,000 Hessians.

It has been customary to be rather contemptuous of the

The German soldiers hired by the British to fight in the Revolution were overloaded with equipment, but proved to be brave, tough fighting men.
NEW YORK PUBLIC LIBRARY PICTURE COLLECTION

HESSIAN SOLDIER.

Germans in the Revolution, chiefly because Washington caught the Hessians off guard at Trenton while they were sleeping off their drunken Christmas celebration, and gave them a terrible beating. But the Hessians, Brunswickers, Waldeckers and Hanoverians hired by the British to fight in the Revolution were skilled professional soldiers. While war for them was a business and not a struggle for freedom or preservation of their government's power, they were brave, bold, doggedly determined soldiers who gave King George III of Britain every penny of his money's worth.

Of the three British generals who had come to Boston to help General Gage, only Howe and Henry Clinton took part in the New York campaign. Burgoyne, unhappy in Boston, had gone back to England. Although Burgoyne was itching for a chance to distinguish himself, he had been forced to watch the battle of Bunker Hill from Copp's Hill across the Charles River. He wrote that he thought he was sent to Boston for some other purpose than "to see that the soldiers boiled their kettles regularly."

General Howe now had 32,000 trained, disciplined soldiers, many of them veterans of European wars, plus arms of all kinds including many cannon, vast stores of ammunition and other equipment as well as ample food supplies. There were ten great ships-of-the-line, mounting altogether more than six hundred guns, twenty somewhat smaller frigates with twice as many cannon, and over 10,000 seamen. Here were an army and fleet that seemed invincible against Washington's meager force of 19,000 untrained soldiers.

Nevertheless, Washington was determined to meet the

British invasion. New York was infested with Tories, and other citizens were waiting to support the British if they conquered the city. A smashing British victory might easily take what was now called the State of New York under the newly-signed Declaration of Independence out of the Revolution and make it a British colony again.

Washington knew the British would undoubtedly march as far as possible by land, to the western end of Long Island and cross the East River to Manhattan Island while Admiral Howe's big guns pounded the city from offshore. Everything was favorable to such an approach. Long Island was a nest of Tories who would help the redcoats in any way they could. Furthermore, most of Long Island was flat, which would make the British march relatively easy. Near the western end, however, there were low heights, including a ridge crossing most of the island there from north to south.

Washington intended to use those elevations to stand off and at least delay the British army's progress as long as possible while inflicting heavy casualties. He sent his most trusted general, Nathanael Greene, to what is now Brooklyn to prepare strong defenses there.

Greene is considered the second greatest American general of the Revolution, if Benedict Arnold is omitted from the reckoning. As a brigadier general he had marched his Rhode Island contingent into Cambridge and then set up his camp at nearby Jamaica Plain. His men were neat, well-trained and obedient, and his camp was a model of order and cleanliness with as much comfort as was possible under the wretched conditions that prevailed.

Many American officers were so disheartened over the prospects of winning the siege of Boston that they made

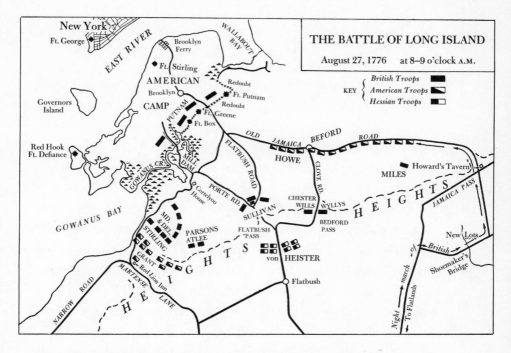

The positions of Gen. Howe's and the American armies and the routes followed by the British in the battle of Long Island.

no effort to improve their troops' military ability or their housing conditions. Hearing of Nathanael Greene's efforts to make his camp livable and to better his soldiers' fighting powers, they came there to jeer and stayed to ask Greene how they might accomplish the same kind of miracle.

Greene went at his task on Long Island with the same sort of thoroughness, traveling over its western end until he knew every inch of it and its best possibilities for defense. Under his direction a series of forts and outworks, interconnected by trenches, was set up.

If Nathanael Greene had been there, the story of the battle of Long Island might have been different. But at the last moment he was stricken with a serious fever, and had to be removed to a hospital in Manhattan, where he nearly died.

Maj. Gen. Israel Putnam replaced Greene in command on Long Island. "Old Put" was a great patriot and a skilled, long-experienced Indian fighter in the colonial wars, but he was no expert at tactics and strategy in this type of battle. Unlike General Greene, he knew little of the terrain of western Long Island.

On August 22, 1776, General Howe landed 15,000 troops with artillery, equipment and supplies at Gravesend Bay on Long Island. General Clinton had set up the plan of attack, which was a three-pronged assault on the American defenses. Maj. Gen. James Grant would avoid the protecting ridge by leading 5,000 redcoats along a route skirting the shore of the harbor, then striking northward. Maj. Gen. Philip von Heister with his Hessians would push toward the center of the American lines, while Howe would lead 10,000 troops toward the left or northern end of the enemy's defenses.

There were roads leading through three passes in the ridge separating the oncoming British from the Americans. The two known as the Bedford and Flatbush passes were well guarded by American detachments, but for some reason never properly explained, the third one was protected by only five young militiamen. The strongest British force of 10,000, commanded by Howe, accompanied by Clinton and Gen. Earl Charles Cornwallis, was to follow this third route, the Jamaica Pass.

At nine o'clock on the evening of August 26, Clinton led the van of the 10,000 redcoats over the road to the Jamaica Pass. They advanced with great caution until, between two and three o'clock on the morning of August 22, Clinton, having made a roundabout approach to the pass, surrounded and captured the five American militiamen. The 10,000 British soldiers then poured through the pass.

They soon met somewhat stronger opposition. Col. Samuel Miles of a Pennsylvania regiment, for another not fully explained reason, became worried about the Jamaica Pass and set out for it with 500 men. Nevertheless, the British captured Miles and a large part of his force.

Meanwhile, General Grant's 5,000 British troops, taking the shore route, overcame an American picket post in the darkness before sunrise. But he met stiff opposition from the right wing of the American lines, where he was kept from advancing farther for four hours, until 2,000 British reinforcements came up to join him.

General Grant, when he was a Member of Parliament before coming to America, had boasted that with 5,000 men he could march from one end of the American continent to the other. Maj. Gen. William Stirling, who claimed to be a Scottish earl, but was fighting for the Americans, pointed to a nearby pond and said to his men: "He may have 5,000 with him now. We are not so many. But I think we are enough to prevent his advancing further on his march over the continent than that millpond."

The words were bold, but the British superiority of numbers prevailed at last. Stirling was forced to retreat when Cornwallis, who had come through the Jamaica Pass, circled around to his rear. For a time the Americans fought desperately, but finally had to surrender.

As a result of the British breakthrough at the Jamaica Pass, the Americans at the Flatbush and Bedford passes under command of Maj. Gen. John Sullivan suddenly found that General Clinton's soldiers were behind them as they faced the Hessian attack at the American center. Caught in the trap, Sullivan's men broke and fled; he and several hundred survivors of this engagement were captured.

When General Washington, in Manhattan, learned that the Long Island forces were taking a disastrous beating, he resolved he would somehow save those who were not already out of action or captured. He sent reinforcements over to cover the American retreat and came to Long Island himself and took command.

It was then about noon, and the battle was over. The Americans had lost about 1,500 men and the British had won the battle with a loss of only about 400—a low price for a victory that could have wiped out the whole Ameri-

American Maj. Gen. William Stirling made a gallant but hopeless stand against the victorious British at the battle of Long Island.
NEW YORK PUBLIC LIBRARY PICTURE COLLECTION

can army on Long Island. Washington's troops there were
so disorganized that they would have been Howe's for the
taking if he had launched another assault that afternoon.
The redcoats were eager for another attack; Howe himself reported that it required "repeated orders to prevail
upon them to desist from this attempt."

But instead, Howe withdrew his army to a safe distance
from the American works and their cannon. Why did he do
it when 8,500 Americans were within his grasp? Many
historians believe he was thinking of his disastrous victory
at Bunker Hill, and he himself said he "would not risk the
loss that might have been sustained in the assault." Howe
added that it seemed apparent the Americans could have
been taken "at a very cheap rate by regular approaches."

Unlike Breed's Hill, there was no steep height to be
surmounted, and the Americans left to fight were too
disorganized to put up a real battle. Howe did not capture them by "regular approaches," although he had two
days to do it, and the Americans managed to hold their
lines against some half-hearted British assaults.

Howe gained another advantage when it poured for two
whole days, and the American camp became a morass with
guns and ammunition soaked and useless, while the British, with their tents, could keep their weapons and powder
dry. But still Howe did not launch an assault that would
have overrun his enemy.

Washington decided the remaining American troops
must be evacuated across the East River to Manhattan.
Every possible boat along the shore was rounded up. To
keep the British unaware of the withdrawal, a regiment
from Delaware, two from Pennsylvania, the remnants of

one from Maryland and a battalion from Connecticut were given the dangerous task of manning the defense lines until the removal of the rest was completed.

The evacuation was accomplished during the night of August 29–30 in craft manned by skilled boatmen from the seafaring town of Marblehead, Massachusetts. It was four in the morning before the brave men still guarding the defense lines were ordered to leave.

Half an hour later the British learned what was afoot. They reached the East River shore a little before seven, just as the last boat, with Washington in it, was pulling away. The redcoats opened fire with muskets and one field gun, but their aim was bad and they scored no hits.

Washington's strategy and skill were the shining light of the withdrawal from Long Island. But for Washington, William Howe might have captured the rest of the Long Island army and Washington himself, and if he had, in all probability the American Revolution would have been over.

6

Manhattan and the Interrupted Chase

GENERAL HOWE HAS BEEN BLAMED FOR MISSING A GREAT chance to crush the American Revolution after the battle of Long Island. He then waited more than two weeks before landing his army on Manhattan September 15, 1776. Even though Washington had succeeded in reorganizing his shattered troops and in throwing up more defenses during that breathing spell, the Americans were weakened, having lost three or four hundred captured, as well as many deserters when the British landed in New York City. Howe dallied and failed to catch them before they reached a good defensive position at Harlem Heights in northern Manhattan. Washington's army was too small to oppose the British, and ridden with desertions, including whole companies at once, with insubordination, mutiny, theft and cowardice under fire. But it was mid-November before Howe captured 2,600 Americans when he took Fort Washington in northern Manhattan and thus gained full control of the island, including what was then New York City at Manhattan's southern end.

Howe's movements, while they were probably too cautious, were good military strategy, whereas the tactics of the American generals were bad. Howe has been criticized for not catching and destroying the enemy, who were running helter-skelter northward for their lives. Indeed, he stopped and camped on Murray Hill, today in midtown Manhattan, which in 1776 was placid countryside.

There is a charming story that has been repeated many times about how a patriotic Quaker lady who lived on Murray Hill delayed Howe and saved the American army. She was Mrs. Robert Murray, one of the family for which the hill was named.

It was a sizzling hot day in September when General Howe and his army reached Mrs. Murray's house. He accepted her invitation for him and his staff to stop, rest and refresh themselves with cakes and wine.

The story that they did stop, rest and were regaled with food and drink is true enough, but Mrs. Murray's hospitality did not actually save the American army. Howe would have stopped to wait anyway until his army's main body of about 9,000 joined him, wanting to avoid any more Bunker Hills.

Exhausted by heat and hurry, the Americans reached Harlem Heights ahead of Howe. The plateau on the narrow northern neck of Manhattan island was a good position for defense because of its elevation. The troops put up redoubts connected by trenches. Washington had 10,000 men on Harlem Heights out of an army of a little over 16,000 who were fit for duty; the rest he sent across the Harlem to Kingsbridge in what is today the Bronx.

The British camped at the southern end of the plateau.

The Americans fleeing from New York City turned and fought
fiercely against the British at Harlem Heights.

Howe's wisdom in waiting for his entire army was proved
when what started out as a skirmish between about 150
Connecticut rangers on a scouting expedition and a few
redcoats turned into a real battle. Both sides sent in
reinforcements until about 5,000 troops were engaged on
each side. In spite of their miserable showing against the
enemy in New York City, the Americans resisted Howe's
men with ferocity. When they were finally forced to retire
a short distance, the British, whose losses were much
heavier than those of Washington's men, did not follow.
Although the battle of Harlem Heights can be called
a British victory, it cheered the Americans greatly to find
they could stand up against trained fighting men.

After the battle of Harlem Heights, Howe learned that
he had an enemy that could be dangerous, and therefore
took his time in making plans for his next move. He

remained in his Harlem Heights camp for twenty-six days and on October 12 his troops embarked in eighty vessels of all kinds and went up Long Island Sound to Throg's Neck. Throg's Neck today is a peninsula sticking out into Long Island Sound, but in 1776 the tip of the neck was an island, cut off by marshes and a creek and a bad place to land troops, as General Howe was to discover.

There was a bridge over the creek, but twenty-five American riflemen had ripped up its planks and built a concealing shelter from behind which they repulsed the whole van of the British army. Then Washington sent in 1,800 reinforcements. Realizing that floundering through the marshes and crossing the creek under heavy enemy fire would be reckless, Howe camped for six more days to wait for his baggage and supplies from New York City.

Howe's purpose was a flanking movement to get around to the rear of the American camp on Harlem Heights. Washington countered it by moving his army north to White Plains. But he left 2,000 soldiers to hold Fort Washington, just north of the Harlem Heights camp. This was a bad military decision since it divided his army into two parts, with fifteen miles between them. In that decision, made by Nathanael Greene, now a major general, lay disaster. It was the first and only serious mistake of his entire military career. He told General Washington that the fort could be held against the British, and the commander in chief accepted his advice.

When Howe was ready to move again he advanced by the better route of Pell's Point, north of Throg's Neck. He met American opposition, but was able to move on north, and on October 28, 1776, the battle of White Plains took place. The Americans fought well, but were defeated and forced to withdraw still farther north. Now General Howe was ready to storm Fort Washington.

General Washington did not know in which direction Howe would move. He left 7,000 men up the Hudson at North Castle to block any British advance upon Albany, and 4,000 men above them near Peekskill to guard the Hudson Highlands. Although the American commander in chief had little choice, this was poor defensive strategy—the American army was thus split into four parts, with the fourth, under Washington himself, at Fort Lee on the New Jersey side of the Hudson directly across from Fort Washington. And with winter coming on his men were wretchedly equipped for bitter weather.

On the morning of November 16, from the top of the Palisades near Fort Lee, Washington, Greene and Putnam watched the British assault on Fort Washington with growing alarm and dismay. Howe's plan of attack was excellent. The fort was to be assaulted from three directions by 8,000 troops—3,000 Germans from the north across the Harlem River, two columns totaling another 3,000 to strike from the east, and 2,000 British and Hessians to move up from the south. Howe did not consider the west side of the fort because there was almost a sheer drop of over two hundred feet down the cliffs to the Hudson shore.

When the British attacked, things did not go smoothly at first. The force of 2,000 advanced without much trouble from the south, pushing back the American outpost defenders there. But when their commander, Earl Hugh Percy, learned that the two columns striking from the east

were having trouble, he halted so that they and his force
could attack at the same time.

The Germans, advancing from the north, did better. It
was the hardest assault of the three because the northern
end of Manhattan was wild, rocky and cut up by ravines.
There was fierce American resistance there too. However,
the mercenaries did manage to gain a foothold on the
heights to the north of the fort.

Then, to their consternation, Washington, Greene and
Putnam, on the opposite side of the river, saw a column of
Hessians emerge on the Hudson shore, move a short distance downstream and then strike directly up the cliffs
toward the fort. The Americans fought against them
fiercely, pouring a deadly hail of lead down upon the
Hessians, who were scrambling, clawing and pulling themselves up through the brush on the cliffs. Many tumbled
back down, dead or wounded, but the Americans fired
their volleys so fast that many of their muskets became
overheated and useless.

Taking advantage of the slackened American fire, Col.
Johann Rall's Hessian regiment surmounted the height
and demanded the fort's surrender. Col. Robert Magaw of
the fort's garrison saw that with the other enemy columns
advancing on him, further resistance would only sacrifice
his men's lives needlessly, and so he surrendered Fort
Washington. Every man of the garrison, which had been
reinforced to about 2,600 men, was killed, wounded or
captured. This was a tougher kind of Bunker Hill, but the
rewards were far greater for the British.

The battle was an American catastrophe for which
General Washington as commander in chief publicly took

the blame. He had had serious doubts about the possibility of holding the fort, but he left the decision up to Nathanael Greene. In London, when the news of Howe's achievements in New York arrived, George III decided to confer knighthood upon his commander in America by making him a Knight Commander of the Bath.

A second American calamity followed shortly after when General Washington decided to defend Fort Lee with its garrison of 3,000. If Howe had started immediately with his superior strength he could have captured Fort Lee, the demoralized garrison, and the large amount of equipment and supplies there. However, he delayed for three days to give his army, which had fought a fierce and exhausting battle, a little rest. Washington then changed his mind and decided that Fort Lee, without its companion, Fort Washington, on the New York side of the river, was of no strategic importance. His decision was nearly too late, for although the soldiers at Fort Lee did miraculously escape, the enemy was almost at their shirttails.

On the night of November 19, General Cornwallis, with

Lord Cornwallis, an able British general, was nearly always chasing the Americans and not catching up with them during the Revolution.
NEW YORK PUBLIC LIBRARY PICTURE COLLECTION

about 4,000 British and Hessians, crossed the Hudson and landed five or six miles above Fort Lee. It was raining very heavily, but they sloshed on through puddles and mud. Early in the morning an American patrol officer sighted the enemy and woke Nathanael Greene at the fort, who notified Washington.

There was no time to prepare to fight. The men got out of Fort Lee in a hurry, leaving behind them three hundred badly needed tents, the fort's thirty cannon, twenty-eight hundred muskets, ammunition, equipment, a thousand barrels of flour and other food. The British found the soldiers' breakfast camp kettles boiling over the fires.

Cornwallis' men gave chase to the panic-stricken Americans. Although Nathanael Greene rode back to round up three hundred stragglers in the rear and try to get them to safety, the redcoats captured 105 of them and killed a few.

Once again General Howe had the chance to clinch a victory that could well have ended the Revolution. He controlled Long Island, Manhattan and the territory just to the north of the island. Ahead of him a terrified and disorganized American army was in flight. Washington was now in the worst straits of the war up to that time, with the rest of his army up the Hudson, too far away to be of immediate aid. All Howe had to do was to catch Washington and his men. He sent Cornwallis on ahead to capture or destroy his prey, and poured more troops into New Jersey behind this advance force.

Washington, desperately needing more men, felt that Maj. Gen. Charles Lee's 7,000 troops upriver at North Castle could be spared from guarding the Hudson since there were other troops up at the Highlands, and wrote Lee strongly urging him to come to his aid. Lee was a strange character, ambitious, disagreeable and not always trustworthy. Since Washington's letter was not a direct order, Lee disregarded it for a time, and when he did march it was too late to help the commander in chief.

Howe was so sure he had Washington and his broken Americans, along with the Revolution itself, in his pocket, that he sent 6,000 of his troops under Clinton to Rhode Island, which they captured with ease.

Washington, meanwhile, was using every possible means of obtaining reinforcements. He appealed to the New Jersey militia, but they did not come. The Continental Congress in Philadelphia had Pennsylvania volunteers on the way, but they had not arrived. To make matters worse, Cornwallis was hot on Washington's heels. The Americans barely got out of Newark ahead of him and on to New Brunswick, which General Stirling had reached with the American vanguard. Washington's problems increased on November 30, when 2,000 men from Maryland and New Jersey, whose enlistments had expired, went home.

On December 1, Cornwallis reached the Raritan River, just across from New Brunswick, where Washington and the remnants of his army were. The Americans had destroyed the bridge there, but at several places nearby Cornwallis could easily have forded the river, caught up with the exhausted Americans and destroyed them. Instead, he waited on the far side for four days, having received orders to wait until Howe and the main army caught up with him.

At Trenton the Hessians, sleeping off their traditional Christmas celebration, were surprised and captured by Washington's army Dec. 26, 1776. YALE UNIVERSITY ART GALLERY

When Howe arrived, the British went on. Just as Cornwallis, leading the van, reached the Delaware River, the last of the boats carrying Washington's army were pushing off. Every sort of craft for miles along the river had been commandeered by the Americans. Cornwallis could only watch the enemy being rowed to safety on the Pennsylvania shore.

Washington's reinforced and rested army recrossed the Delaware and on the morning of December 26, 1776, fell upon the Hessians Cornwallis had stationed in Trenton with the savagery of men who have been thoroughly beaten and were looking for revenge. Howe was in New

York, celebrating the presentation of the knighthood that made him Sir William Howe.

Sir William seems to have thrown away a sure and devastating victory. His biographer, Bellamy Partridge, suggested a possible explanation. Howe and his brother, Richard Howe, the admiral in the British navy, were staunch members of the Whig Party in England, which had opposed Parliament's measures that had brought on the Revolution, as compared to the Tory Party, which favored them. Both the Howes had arrived in New York on a mission of peace—to negotiate a settlement that the colonies could accept with honor and yet remain a British possession, which would be a great triumph for the Whigs in Parliament. Unfortunately for the Howes, the signing of the Declaration of Independence destroyed their hopes.

According to Partridge's theory, the Howes' plan was to beat the Americans, but not so badly as to humiliate them. Thus the Americans would be more amenable to make peace under liberal British terms. This theory would explain Howe's failure to destroy Washington's army completely when they were within such easy reach. With all of Long Island, Manhattan and New Jersey under his control, Howe was in a position to propose liberal terms. However, he did not foresee the Hessian defeat at Trenton.

7

The Dilatory Dogs of War and the Slippery Fox

IN NEW YORK, GENERAL HOWE WAS UNDERSTANDABLY OUT-raged by the news of Trenton. "That three old established regiments of a people who make war a profession should lay down their arms to a ragged and undisciplined militia is stupefying," he was reported as commenting.

The situation called for Howe to go to New Jersey at once, but he was having too good a time in New York. Cornwallis was just about to sail for England on leave, but Howe sent him to New Jersey.

Washington had taken his army back across the Delaware to Pennsylvania after his victory at Trenton. There were too many units of British troops scattered over New Jersey and he wanted to rest and strengthen his army, before returning.

Brig. Gen. Joseph Reed was leading a scouting force to see just where the British forces were located in New Jersey and what they were up to. Finding that no enemy soldiers had reoccupied Trenton he wrote Washington urging him to come over at once. It was poor advice, but the commander in chief decided not to wait. On December 29 his army began crossing the Delaware once more. When Washington reached the New Jersey side, he learned that Cornwallis, with 8,000 troops and a large train of artillery, was at Princeton, only about a dozen miles away, and beginning an advance upon Trenton.

Washington had only about 1,500 men, and the enlistments of most of his best fighters, the Continental army troops, would expire December 31. Brig. Gen. Thomas Mifflin and Henry Knox, now also a brigadier, made a personal plea to the men, offering them ten dollars extra pay if they would stay six more weeks. More than half accepted, which was remarkable considering that they were paid in the unreliable paper money that Robert Morris raised in Philadelphia on his own credit.

Even then, Washington had a pitiful force to oppose Cornwallis' big, battle-seasoned army. However, Brig. Gen. John Cadwalader was down the Delaware on the Pennsylvania side with 2,100 troops, which he brought over. Mifflin managed to raise 1,600 more militia in Philadelphia, who joined Washington, giving him over 5,000 men and fifty pieces of artillery.

Since Cornwallis left 1,200 men at Princeton, his army was of about the same size as Washington's, but made up of far better fighting men, and while he had only twenty-eight pieces of artillery, some were heavy 12-pounders. There could be no doubt of the British superiority.

On the night of January 2, 1777, as Cornwallis' force approached Trenton it was pouring rain that did not last the night, but had turned the roads into morasses. The ad-

vance units of the mud-soaked British troops were held up
three hours by American outposts which fought them to
a standstill until the main British army came up and
forced them to retire and join Washington's army on the
south side of Assunpink Creek.

Assunpink Creek, a small stream, ran westward along
the southern edge of Trenton and flowed into the Delaware. Washington had placed his army in a line nearly
three miles long on a ridge. The position had one fatal de-
fect: the Americans had the broad Delaware cutting them
off in that direction, and the only roads over which a retreat could be made led toward Princeton. Thus the Americans were neatly trapped between Cornwallis, on the
north bank of the Assunpink, and the British force at
Princeton.

Washington's army swoops down on the groggy Hessians at Trenton.

The advance British force tried three times to cross a bridge over the creek and were driven back, as were some Hessians who tried to wade across at a ford. But once the main British army reached the creek it could hardly be prevented from storming the American defense lines.

Cornwallis held a council with his generals, and Brig. Gen. Sir William Erskine urged him to attack immediately. Cornwallis is supposed to have said: "We've got the old fox safely now. We'll go over and bag him in the morning." Some historians doubt he said it, but as one writer has remarked, no one has ever proved he didn't. Erskine is said to have replied, "If Washington is the general I take him to be, he will not be found there in the morning." But Cornwallis did not agree.

All through that night British sentries saw the American campfires on the long defense line across the creek flare up as they were replenished with fence rails. They could hear the clack and clank of spades and pickaxes that could only mean the enemy was striving desperately to throw up more earthworks. They saw American sentries patrolling the defenses.

The racket drowned out the sound of wagon wheels crunching over the now-frozen road toward Burlington, down the Delaware, as well as the sound of gun-carriage wheels wrapped in cloth to muffle them, as most of the artillery moved toward the safety of Burlington. Nor did the British sentries discover the stealthy withdrawal of the American army, who had left only a skeleton force to tend the fires and deceive the enemy with their entrenching tools. It was near dawn before these few men also withdrew and hurried to catch up with the main American army.

Silently, the Americans marched over a little-used road running through dense woods. Sometime after dawn the vanguard saw a flash of scarlet ahead—a British force on its way from Princeton to join Cornwallis. The British thought the soldiers ahead of them were part of Washington's army fleeing from the expected American defeat at Trenton, but they soon found out they were up against a whole army.

In spite of their surprise, the redcoats fought with such organization and ferocity that the Americans were thrown into a retreat that turned to a disorderly rout. It is appalling to think what would have happened if the Americans actually had been fleeing from Cornwallis and found themselves sandwiched between the two enemy forces. Only Washington's military genius permitted him to rally and reorganize his men and finally inflict a disastrous defeat upon the British column, which fled, leaving many dead and fifty captured behind them.

The commander in chief quickly seized his advantage and pounced on the British who were still in Princeton. Most of the enemy took refuge in Nassau Hall of the College of New Jersey, later to be Princeton University. But the commander of an American artillery battery, young Capt. Alexander Hamilton, who was to become famous as the first United States Secretary of the Treasury, sent a few cannonballs crashing into the building, which brought the enemy scurrying out to surrender.

By Washington's estimates there were 100 British killed and 300 wounded, while the enemy's own claim was 28 killed, 58 wounded and 187 missing. The Americans' report was 40 killed and wounded. The victory at Princeton

After thoroughly outgeneraling Cornwallis at Assunpink Creek, Washington, with his army, scored a sweeping victory at Princeton.

on top of the victory at Trenton was heartening to the colonies. But the most important result was the recognition in Europe, as well as America, of Washington's ability as a general. But if Cornwallis had not delayed the attack during the night of January 2 and 3, the British could well have wiped out Washington's trapped army on the bank of the Assunpink.

8

Burgoyne Makes His First Mistake

AFTER THE BATTLE OF PRINCETON THE BRITISH WENT INTO winter quarters at several points in New Jersey and the Americans settled at Morristown. For the rest of the winter they did little but play tag with each other in a few skirmishes and raids. In New York, Howe, in spite of his vastly superior resources, did nothing except play more amusing games of his own with the hospitable wealthy Tories there.

At this time another British commander was planning a campaign by himself. Maj. Gen. John Burgoyne had been with General Carleton and the British army when they marched within striking distance of Ticonderoga in 1776, but then had to return to Canada because of the bitter winter weather. During the winter of 1776–77, Burgoyne was in England, very busy with an ambitious and similar scheme to finish off the American rebels once and for all.

Burgoyne was by far the most colorful of the British generals in America during the Revolution. He was an able general, except that he had too great a contempt for the

Americans, was far too fond of drinking, gambling and the ladies, and made three disastrous mistakes while leading a British army in America.

Burgoyne's soldiers thought there was no better general in all Britain. He treated his men like human beings instead of dogs, unlike other British officers; in general the only worse existence for an enlisted man in those days was that of a seaman in the British navy. In gratitude, Burgoyne's men affectionately called him "Gentleman Johnny," and by that name he is well known in history.

Burgoyne was not only a "gentleman" in the British sense of the word at that time, coming from a titled family, but he was also always a true gentleman in his behavior. Handsome Burgoyne loved the life of a London man-about-town, and while his parents were poor, he married a rich woman and was able to frequent the best clubs whenever he was in London. By the time the Revolution began he had considerable military service, though not a great deal of fighting experience, and his efficient command of one of George II's favorite regiments had won him the high regard of both that king and his successor, George III.

In fact, about the only man high in the British government who did not like Burgoyne was Lord George Germain, who as Secretary of State for the Colonies was responsible for carrying on the war in America. Germain blamed Burgoyne as well as Carleton for the failure to capture Ticonderoga in 1776. Germain was an arrogant, hot tempered, obstinate man, and but for him, Burgoyne might have shared with Sir William Howe the glory of winning the American Revolution.

Burgoyne had a great plan to win the war which

he wrote about in a pamphlet called "Thoughts for Conducting the War from the Side of Canada." If he had submitted it to Germain, it probably would have been ignored. But Gentleman Johnny took his proposal straight to his friend, the King.

He suggested that an army from Canada should invade the American colonies by the Lake Champlain route, take Ticonderoga and move on south. Although he did not mention it in his report, Burgoyne of course intended to be in command of such an expedition. General Howe would march his army up the Hudson to meet Burgoyne at Albany or somewhere down the river. Thus the previous plan of chopping off the head of the Revolution—New England—would be accomplished. Burgoyne and Howe could then combine and crush Washington.

George III was delighted with the scheme and ordered Germain to see that it was carried out, with Burgoyne in command. Germain wrote General Carleton that Burgoyne was to supersede him in leading the invasion army. He made a few nasty criticisms of Carleton and told him of the plan for Howe to march north to meet Burgoyne,

Sir Guy Carleton, probably the best of the British Revolutionary generals, had little chance to display his talents because of the enmity of Lord George Germain.

NEW YORK PUBLIC LIBRARY PICTURE COLLECTION

saying it was "highly necessary that the most speedy Junction of the two Armies should be effected."

Germain added, "I shall write to Sir William by the next packet." These are most important words to remember as the story of Gentleman Johnny's adventures unfolds. Burgoyne came to Canada with full assurance that Howe would soon be on his way north up the Hudson, according to reliable sources, although one well-known historian claims there was no understanding that Howe would do this.

Carleton was outraged at being displaced by Burgoyne, and he told Germain so in no uncertain terms in a bitter reply to the Colonial Secretary's letter. But Sir Guy was not only as fine a gentleman as Burgoyne, but a splendid officer and staunchly loyal to Britain. When Burgoyne reached Canada, Carleton gave him every possible assistance to make the invasion a success.

Burgoyne's plan called for an army of 8,000 British regulars with plenty of artillery, 2,000 Canadians and a thousand or more Indians. He would leave 3,000 men to guard Canada. A formidable armada was to be provided to carry the rest up Lake Champlain.

Burgoyne arrived at Quebec May 6, 1777. All his expectations were not met, however. The troops in Canada were in good shape, but their uniforms were badly worn and new ones had not come from England. Part of the Canadian contingent consisted of German mercenaries, called Brunswickers. Their ruler, the tight-fisted Duke of Brunswick, who was profiting handsomely from his troops' service in America, had sent them to Canada in uniforms and shoes already badly worn, and by this time they were much worse. The Brunswickers were loaded down with a heavy assortment of equipment that made marching difficult. The Brunswicker dragoons badly needed more wagons for the baggage train and horses, as did Burgoyne.

Instead of the expected large force of Canadian Tories and French Canadians that Burgoyne had been expecting, only 250 had enlisted. As for the Indians, Burgoyne got only 400 out of the expected thousand. Burgoyne's fleet, awaiting him at St. Johns, however, was excellent. He had five good warships used by Carleton the year before, including the powerful *Inflexible* sloop of war mounting eighteen 12-pounder cannon, two armed schooners, a galley propelled by oars and sails and the *Thunderer*, a huge floating platform carrying six great 24-pounders, six 12-pounders and two small howitzers. To these were added three small vessels captured from Arnold the year before, a large warship built during the winter at St. Johns, twenty-eight gunboats and plenty of flat-bottomed bateaux to land troops.

The artillery, including the ships' cannon, amounted to 138 guns, from 3-pounders up to the great 24-pounders. For use in battle in the field, Burgoyne had 42 guns of different sizes.

The first of three serious mistakes Burgoyne made during the campaign was a secondary expedition that began after Gentleman Johnny, his army and armada were well on their way. The expedition was intended to subdue the Mohawk Valley.

The Mohawk River rises west of the Adirondack Mountains, flows south for a time and then, with many twistings and turnings, heads east across New York and flows into the Hudson a little above Albany. The valley was not heavily settled, and although the settlers were about equally divided between Tories and American rebels, the Tories were, however, better organized.

Nevertheless, on his way up the St. Lawrence River, Burgoyne detached about 750 regulars, Tory volunteers, a few French Canadians and artillerymen to handle four light field guns and four mortars. The force was commanded by Lieut. Col. Barry St. Leger, who had been made a temporary brigadier general for the expedition.

It seemed to Burgoyne that taking only about a tenth of his total strength of some 7,400 soldiers away from the main army could scarcely affect its power. He expected that after conquering the Mohawk Valley, St. Leger's men would rejoin the main army at or near Albany.

Barry St. Leger was similar to Burgoyne in his character—a dashing, devil-may-care fellow with the same weakness for wine, women and the gambling table. He cockily anticipated no trouble in sweeping the Mohawk Valley clear of rebel resistance, and once this was accomplished, his important temporary promotion would doubtless be made permanent. There was only one major defense work in his path, Fort Stanwix, near present-day Rome, New York, and his information was that this relic of the colonial wars was crumbling, occupied by only a handful of American rebels and should be easy to take.

Burgoyne was not depending solely upon those 750 troops but expected that the Tories of the region would flock to join St. Leger, as well as a thousand Indians of the powerful Six Nations of Iroquois, led by the Mohawk chief Joseph Brant, whose Indian name was

Thayendanegea. Brant was not only seasoned by fighting in the French and Indian War, but one of the most brilliant Indian leaders in American history.

St. Leger's force assembled at Lachine, just above Montreal, went on up the St. Lawrence and into Lake Ontario as far as Oswego. There Joseph Brant and about a thousand of his warriors joined them. The army started July 26, 1777. And although they had to march eastward through a wilderness of swamps, streams and forest carrying their artillery and baggage, they were able to advance in perfect order, making a remarkable ten miles a day.

But St. Leger did not know that Fort Stanwix had been occupied by a Continental regiment under energetic Col. Peter Gansevoort. He and his equally competent second in command, Lieut. Col. Marinus Willett, had put their men to work restoring the ancient fort into a formidable defensive work. St. Leger learned that 200 reinforcements and supplies were on their way to Stanwix from the east, and so he sent a contingent to intercept and destroy the force but they were too late. The new American detachment got safely into the fort.

Nor did St. Leger learn until later that Brig. Gen. Nicholas Herkimer of the New York militia was headed toward Fort Stanwix with 800 volunteers. Herkimer was the son of a German immigrant, and like many other settlers in the valley spoke German better than English. He was a veteran of the French and Indian War, a staunch patriot and a tough fighter.

St. Leger arrived at Fort Stanwix on August 8, and sent in a message demanding surrender. The demand was sheer bluff, for St. Leger realized that the fort was too strong to be taken by storm. When the Americans did not even bother to answer the summons, St. Leger prepared to besiege the fort.

Herkimer had sent scouts ahead to tell Colonel Gansevoort that if he was ready to send troops out of the fort when Herkimer's men approached he should fire three cannon shots. When none were heard, Herkimer decided to wait, but his officers were so determined to push on that they insinuated their commander was a coward. Finally Herkimer yielded and advanced, a decision that proved unfortunate to him personally.

Heroic Brig. Gen. Nicholas Herkimer, with a bullet wound of which he later died, calmly sat under a tree and directed the American victory at Oriskany. NEW YORK PUBLIC LIBRARY PICTURE COLLECTION

St. Leger's Indian scouts reported Herkimer's advance and the British commander set up an ambush in a steep-sided ravine, fifty feet deep with a swampy stream flowing through it. As Herkimer's force marched toward this murderous trap, St. Leger left the east end of the ravine open. He posted part of his army in a half circle around the western end, with the Indians concealed in the forest behind it. Once Herkimer's men were in the ravine the Indians would encircle it, closing the jaws of the trap.

For some reason, Herkimer's Indian scouts, who were Oneidas, one of two Six Nations tribes who had not sided with the British, did not discover the ambush. In a fierce, hand-to-hand battle the startled Americans clubbed their muskets against the bayonets of St. Leger's white men and the tomahawks of the Indians. A British bullet shattered Herkimer's leg and his horse was shot dead under him. Although the situation seemed hopeless for the Americans, Herkimer was too experienced a fighter at this kind of warfare to lose his head. Unable to walk, he calmly sat down under a tree, lit his pipe and directed the battle.

They fought savagely for three-quarters of an hour, got an hour's rest when a violent rainstorm wet their muskets' priming, and went at it again when the sun came out. Herkimer had his men take cover behind trees in twos so that one could reload while the other fired. Such heavy casualties were inflicted upon St. Leger's horde of Indians that the red men retreated into the forest.

Soon St. Leger's white men, mostly Tories, also gave up. Meanwhile, during the battle, Marinus Willett with 250 men sallied out of Fort Stanwix, fell upon the almost deserted camp of the British ambush force, looted it of provisions, arms, ammunition and equipment before destroy-

As this scene shows, the fight at Oriskany was bloody and brutal.

ing it. Thus the Americans turned almost sure defeat into victory at the battle of Oriskany, named after a nearby village.

Exact losses in the battle are not known, but the Americans suffered heavily, probably losing between 150 and 200 dead and 50 wounded, while the enemy killed and wounded are believed to have been about 150. Brave General Herkimer died later of the bullet wound in his leg.

St. Leger then returned to begin his siege of Fort Stanwix. First he sent a party into the fort under a flag of truce. The emissaries said St. Leger's Indians could not be controlled and that unless the fort surrendered immediately the savages would not only massacre everyone in it, but every white man, woman and child in the Mohawk Valley. Gansevoort would not even talk with the emissaries, but had Marinus Willett give them a blistering reply to carry to St. Leger, scornfully condemning the supposedly civilized British commander for making such a threat.

Meanwhile, news of St. Leger's expedition reached General Schuyler at Stillwater, on the Hudson, headquarters of the Northern Continental army. Although he needed all the men he could get to stand off the approaching Burgoyne in a major battle, he said to his officers, "Gentlemen, I shall take the responsibility upon myself. Fort Stanwix and the Mohawk Valley shall be saved! Where is the brigadier who will command the relief?" Benedict Arnold instantly stepped forward and volunteered. Although he knew that St. Leger had 1,700 men in the Mohawk Valley, Arnold took only 950 volunteers and 100 militiamen with him.

Arnold's keen mind devised a plan by which he hoped to trick the British commander. A cunning German settler in the valley, Hon Yost, had been condemned to death for trying to recruit men for the British. Arnold promised him a pardon if he would carry out a mission, and the German agreed. Before leaving, Hon Yost took off his coat, and several bullets were fired through it.

Accompanied by an Oneida, he set out for St. Leger's camp, where he told a tale of having escaped American captivity and showed his bullet-ridden coat. Whether St. Leger believed the story is doubtful, since Yost was a queer character, probably insane, but the Indians were convinced when the Oneida confirmed the German's tale. Two hundred of Joseph Brant's men fled at once, and the remaining chiefs demanded a retreat. St. Leger's army made its way back to Oswego, and Burgoyne would not see them again.

9

Burgoyne's Second Mistake

THE TAKEOFF POINT FOR GENTLEMAN JOHNNY'S GREAT invasion was St. Johns, on the Richelieu River, only a few miles below where it flows northward out of Lake Champlain and joins the St. Lawrence.

Burgoyne wanted to impress the Americans. On June 13, 1777, he had the royal standard—the battle flag of Britain—set up on the *Thunderer*. The banner was magnificent with its symbolic golden lions of England, the Scottish red lion, the Irish harp and the golden fleurs-de-lis of France, where England had once had a firm hold. When the standard was raised, all ships of the invasion fleet ashore fired their cannon in salute.

Burgoyne was not satisfied with this show of might to frighten the rebellious Americans. He took a week more to write and publish a manifesto to them. In spite of Gentleman Johnny's undoubted ability as a playwright, his pronouncement was incredibly windy and pompous. He audaciously claimed that the Revolution had "been made a foundation for the completest system of tyranny that ever God in his displeasure suffered for a time to be exercised over a froward and stubborn generation."

However, the generous British commander offered to protect the inhabitants, "provided they remain quietly in their houses, that they do not suffer their cattle to be removed nor their corn or forage to be secreted or destroyed [this was so that Burgoyne could seize such things to feed his men and horses]; that they do not break up their bridges or roads, nor by any other acts, directly or indirectly, endeavor to obstruct the operations of the King's troops, or supply or subsist those of the enemy. . . ."

Nevertheless, Gentleman Johnny gave the Americans a stern warning: "I have but to give stretch to the Indian forces under my direction (and they amount to thousands) to overtake the hardened enemies of Great Britain and America." His Indians did not amount to thousands, as he very well knew.

Some American patriots were angered by Burgoyne's threats, though not in the least intimidated. Most of them, however, laughed. Humorous verses about Burgoyne and his announcement were published in the American newspapers.

Perhaps because Burgoyne realized he had gone a little too far with his threat to loose his Indians to massacre the inhabitants, he addressed his red men in a speech that was just as pompous as his manifesto to the settlers.

He positively forbade bloodshed by them unless they were opposed by armed force. Also, aged men, and women and children, as well as prisoners, must not be "tomahawked or scalped in battle." Of course, he added, it was all right to take scalps from dead men they themselves had killed in battle, but under no circumstances from dying or wounded soldiers.

In England, when he heard about this speech, Edmund Burke, the great British friend of America, asked the members of Parliament to consider a riot among the animals in the Tower of London, where the Royal Menagerie was then located. Imagine, he asked his hearers, the keeper of the zoo addressing the animals: "My noble lions, my humane bears, my sentimental wolves, my tender-hearted hyenas, go forth: but I exhort ye as ye are Christians and members of a civilized society, to take care not to hurt man, woman or child." A gale of laughter swept the House of Commons.

Although likening the Indians to the Royal Menagerie is an unfortunate comparison, the point Burke was trying to make is valid. The Indians had good cause to hate the colonists who were stealing their land, and to entreat them to be merciful was naive and unrealistic.

Burgoyne's advance force started south on June 20, followed soon afterward by the main army. For some time things went well for the British, so well that Burgoyne could envision nothing but a sweeping victory and the highest honors for himself. He could even relax and enjoy some of the pleasures he loved so well.

The first big objective of Burgoyne's army was Ticonderoga, which was now manned by about 2,500 Americans under command of Maj. Gen. Arthur St. Clair. Indications were that Burgoyne would have no easy time in regaining it as a British possession. But once again a glaring mistake, this time by the Americans under command of Major General Horatio Gates, changed a seemingly easy victory into a defeat.

Although Gates is famous for the great American victory at Saratoga, actually he was incompetent, and Saratoga would have been lost but for Benedict Arnold and Col. Daniel Morgan.

Ticonderoga and its connection to Lake George were vulnerable to cannonades from three hills. About two miles to the northwest rose Mount Hope, commanding the road to Lake George. Across the narrow strait from Ticonderoga was high, steep Mount Independence, from whose summit guns could rain cannonballs directly into the fort. The Americans had taken care to see that both these hills were well fortified, and Burgoyne would not have been foolish enough to try to storm them.

There remained Sugar Loaf, a conical hill 750 feet high, about a mile southwest of Ticonderoga. Before Burgoyne's approach, American engineer officers had strongly recommended that it be fortified. But Gates thought the hill so steep and rocky that no one, American or British, could get guns up there.

When Burgoyne's fleet approached Ticonderoga, Gentleman Johnny took a good look at unfortified Sugar Loaf. Lieutenant Twiss, Burgoyne's chief engineer, reported that Sugar Loaf's northwest flank could not only be climbed, but a road built to the top.

Burgoyne ordered Maj. Gen. William Phillips to see what could be done about it. "Where a goat can go," said Phillips, "a man can go, and where a man can go he can drag a gun." Then he set out to do just that.

When General St. Clair got up on the morning of July

5, 1777, the sun struck out a suspicious flash from the top of Sugar Loaf. Focusing a spyglass on the summit, he spotted British guns on top of the hill commanding Ticonderoga, and redcoats moving about up there.

Here was Dorchester Heights in reverse. St. Clair hastily convened a council of war, and decided they must retreat at nightfall. Luckily, Burgoyne was not yet ready to begin cannonading that day. Under cover of darkness and the roar of Ticonderoga's heavy guns, like Washington's army at Assunpink Creek, St. Clair's force retreated.

It took all night for his army to cross the strait to the New Hampshire Grants side. The American goal was Skenesboro at the southern end of the lake, by a roundabout route, but first they had to cross low-lying, hilly country over a rough, rutted road that made the going slow. The sun came up blazing that morning and the sleepless men sweated in the breathless heat as they plodded on. Then they struck the foothills of the Green Mountains. The road led up a steep hill past the hamlet of Hubbardton.

The British, close on the Americans' heels, occupied the deserted fort. Burgoyne sent Brig. Gen. Simon Fraser with light infantry and grenadiers, in pursuit, followed by Maj. Gen. Friedrich von Riedesel, commander of the expedition's German troops (the American soldiers called him Red Hazel), at the head of a similar force of his Germans.

St. Clair's plan was to descend into the valley to Castleton, then swing west to Skenesboro, and finally reach the safety of the Northern Continental army's camp at Fort Edward on the Hudson. To cover his retreat against the oncoming enemy, he left Col. Seth Warner in command of about 750 men on the Hubbardton hilltop.

Warner was the very opposite of his cousin, Ethan Allen. He was a quiet, unassuming man, a crack shot and an excellent officer, but Warner made a mistake as bad, in a smaller way, as Gates' blunder regarding Sugar Loaf. He neglected to put out pickets while his force camped on the Hubbardton hilltop, thus failing to discover that Fraser's force had camped just down the hill behind the Americans.

While Warner and his men were cooking breakfast the next morning, Fraser's men burst in on them. Despite the surprise attack, Warner did a masterful job of deploying his men and giving the redcoats a fierce battle. The Americans were winning when Riedesel and his Germans, coming up the hill, joined the fight. Even when one of his regiments fled from the field, Warner was able to withdraw the rest in orderly fashion to Castleton.

Hubbardton is an almost forgotten Revolutionary battle, and few people know it was the only battle fought inside what is modern Vermont. Bennington, a much more famous fight, actually took place across today's New York State border. The battle of Hubbardton was important because it delayed Fraser and Riedesel long enough so that when St. Clair's force heard the distant popping of musketry they were able to slip out of Castleton, followed by Warner's swiftly retreating force, reach Skenesboro and then, by a roundabout route, get safely to Fort Edward.

Meanwhile, Burgoyne's main army at Ticonderoga blew to pieces an enormous iron chain and log boom, as well as a bridge with twenty-two obstructing piers that the

Americans had thrown across the narrow strait. The way was now open for Burgoyne's fleet to sail on south.

Ahead of the British ships, a large American flotilla, loaded with as many stores and artillery as could be gotten out of Ticonderoga before the British swarmed in, was making a leisurely way toward Skenesboro. It does not seem to have occurred to the commander that the British could destroy that enormous blocking log boom and chain. He was badly mistaken, of course, and Burgoyne's fleet nearly caught the Americans, who barely reached Skenesboro in time to set the vessels and their precious cargo afire to prevent their capture and then move with all speed toward Fort Edward.

Considering his progress, Burgoyne felt he could afford a little rest before moving on to crush the Northern Continental army. At Skenesboro he found a willing host, Col. Philip Skene, who was well equipped to entertain him.

Skene has been earlier mentioned as a sort of wilderness English lord of the manor in colonial style. Skene was a tall, dignified, suave, handsome man, affable, with quick wits and a sharp tongue. Born in London, he served for years in the British army and distinguished himself in the French and Indian War in America.

When that war ended he bought and obtained grants of a large amount of land at the head of Lake Champlain. He induced thirty families of settlers to live on his land, and named the place Skenesboro. Skene operated a forge, iron works and several other mills there.

Burgoyne found Skene's house most comfortable. The place was well furnished, well stocked with provisions, wines and spirits, and fresh game and fish were available in abundance. Skene, his family, and frequent guests were served by a corps of black slaves.

Burgoyne arrived at Skenesboro July 9, 1777. It was the 25th before he moved on. Within the next three weeks two events took place that were of immeasurable importance in sealing his doom. The first concerned one of the most famous women in Revolutionary history—Jane McCrea.

While Burgoyne was lolling at Skenesboro, General Schuyler was at Fort Edward with only about 2,000 troops, some 1,400 of them militia. The fort was practically a ruin that could not possibly be defended. However, Schuyler's hope was to delay Burgoyne long enough to strengthen the American army.

Burgoyne's route to Fort Edward was over a road running up Wood Creek. The road passed through bogs where at some points causeways would have to be built to get the wagons and artillery through, and it crossed bridges over forty deep ravines.

Although the road was bad anyway, after a thousand men sent out by Schuyler got through with their task, every bridge was in ruins. The road was choked with huge boulders rolled down the hillsides. Great trees on each side of the road had been felled across it in a monumental tangle. Schuyler's men had even dug ditches to carry water from the swamps to flood the road.

The Americans had also warned the inhabitants along the route to drive their cattle off to a distance and either hide or remove what stores of food and forage they had. The march to Fort Edward was going to be a hungry as well as a slow one for Burgoyne's army.

Nevertheless, Gentleman Johnny's Canadian woodsmen

The tomahawking and scalping of Jane McCrea brought
hundreds of American volunteers rushing to enlist before
the battle of Saratoga.

cleared the road, but it took until July 25 before Burgoyne could march the seven miles to abandoned Fort Ann, where there he had to wait four more days before advancing the last sixteen miles to Fort Edward. He found it deserted, since Schuyler had withdrawn his army farther south from the dilapidated fort.

Burgoyne's mistake in delaying too long at Skenesboro was compounded during those four days at Fort Ann by an occurrence that was far more devastating to his plans.

Jane McCrea, twenty-three years old, had been living with her brother, since her mother had died and her father, a New Jersey minister, had married again. The brother had settled on the Hudson River between Fort Edward and Saratoga. With Burgoyne's approach, he decided to move to Albany, but Jane refused to go with him. She was engaged to marry David Jones, a Tory who had fled to Canada, joined Burgoyne's army and was with the invasion force. Jane, wanting to meet her fiancé when he arrived at Fort Edward, went to Fort Edward village and stayed with an old woman, a Mrs. McNeil, who lived in a cabin there.

On July 27, while Burgoyne's army was making its way from Fort Ann to Fort Edward, a group of Indians swooped down on the village. They seized Jane McCrea and Mrs. McNeil and started toward Fort Ann. On the way a dispute arose between two of the savages as to which should be Jane's guard. One of them, conveniently overlooking Burgoyne's pious orders not to harm civilians, shot Jane McCrea dead and scalped her.

The Indians took Mrs. McNeil and Jane's scalp toward Fort Ann. When they met the British army, Burgoyne was appalled and ordered the murderer's arrest and execution. But his Indians were under the command of a white man, Saint Luc de la Corne, a French Canadian and a thorough rascal who had strong influence over the savages. He told Burgoyne that if the murderer were executed, every Indian in the camp would go home. Burgoyne then had the misjudgment to pardon Wyandot Panther, the murderer.

Although Gentleman Johnny felt he needed the Indians' support, if he could have foreseen the storm that would break over his head he would have hanged the murderer and let the red men go. The news of Jane McCrea's scalping spread through the northern American colonies, and became a rallying point for the patriots.

In defense of Burgoyne's Indians it can only be said that scalping in warfare was a way of life for the red men. Many an Indian was scalped by one of his own race in intertribal wars. What happened to Jane McCrea was the act of a particularly violent savage, but murders just as brutal were committed by white men. The blame lies with Burgoyne for thinking he could control his warrior allies.

This was not the first time that Burgoyne's Indians had tomahawked and scalped harmless settlers in that region. Strangely enough since Jane McCrea was engaged to one of Burgoyne's Tory officers, her sympathies must have been with the British, but this made no difference to the outraged patriot settlers. Volunteers flocked in droves to the Northern Continental army's camp to add desperately needed strength for the coming clash with Burgoyne.

During this period, Horatio Gates and Schuyler had

been struggling against each other for command of the northern army. Since Gates had stronger political influence with the Continental Congress in Philadelphia, he had won out, and on August 19 took over command from the far more competent Schuyler. After the final battle of Saratoga on October 7, 1777, Schuyler's wretched army of 2,000 at Fort Edward had grown to 11,000 men under Gates, many having come in response to Jane McCrea's scalping.

10

"Hangs Like a Gathering Storm..."

BY THE TIME BURGOYNE REACHED FORT EDWARD IT WAS essential that he obtain horses, wagons, food and forage, and therefore he resolved to send an expedition to the New Hampshire Grants to get them.

Burgoyne had no personal knowledge of the country-side there and its people, but General Riedesel, who had been there during the chase after St. Clair, was against the expedition. At Hubbardton he had met a formidable enemy in Seth Warner's men of the Grants. The strongest evidence points to Colonel Skene as the one who gave Burgoyne misleading information about the people of that region.

Colonel Skene, who accompanied Burgoyne and the army to Fort Edward, is believed to have urged the British commander to send a corps to ransack the New Hampshire Grants as far as the Connecticut River. He is also said to have told Burgoyne he would obtain recruits there, since the Tories outnumbered the patriot Grants settlers five to one.

Skene should have known better. Ethan Allen and his Green Mountain Boys had chased out many of the "Yorker" settlers, who were inclined to be loyal to Britain, and since then others had found it safer to leave the Grants and had joined the British. Skene also failed to warn Burgoyne about the fighting ability of the Grants farmers who were expert shots from long practice in hunting game.

Skene and Ethan Allen were old friends and drinking companions. During the trouble over the land grants, Skene had supported neither side until he could see how things would turn out, fearing that his estate in Skenesboro might be seized and perhaps destroyed by the Green Mountain Boys if he openly sided with the Yorkers.

Now he was faced with the same problem. Skenesboro could suffer the same fate, since it lay in Burgoyne's rear; a force from the Grants might easily sally out toward Burgoyne's rear and wreck his house, mills and other property on the way. But if Burgoyne invaded and conquered the Grants, Skene's estate would be safe. The most reasonable explanation for Skene's eagerness for Burgoyne to invade the Grants was his desire to protect Skenesboro and his property.

So he volunteered and was accepted to go along with the expedition as a guide and in order to tell "the good subjects from the bad."

Lieut. Col. Friedrich Baum was to lead the force. Yet since it was to recruit Tories for Burgoyne's army, the choice of a German commander who spoke not a word of English seems somewhat odd. There would be about 650 men, including 170 Brunswick dragoons on foot, 100 Ger-

Gen. Stark leads his army in the assault on the hill held by
German Lieut. Col. Baum at the battle of Bennington.
NEW YORK PUBLIC LIBRARY PICTURE COLLECTION

man grenadiers and jäger marksmen, 300 Tories, Canadians and Indians, 50 British marksmen, and artillerymen
to handle the two little 3-pounder field guns.

While preparations for the march were being made in
the British camp, the "peasants," as Colonel Skene called
them, of the New Hampshire Grants were not idle. Ever
since the Hubbardton battle, the farmers had been worried that Burgoyne would raid the Grants. An appeal was
sent to New Hampshire, which appointed John Stark a
brigadier general in command of about 1,500 officers and
men and sent them to Bennington.

Stark was a topnotch officer and fighting man who had
distinguished himself in the French and Indian War. In
1775, he had hurried to Cambridge the moment he heard

the news of Lexington and Concord, fought at Bunker
Hill, participated in the unsuccessful invasion of Canada
in 1775 and 1776 and the ensuing battles at Trenton and
Princeton. But he saw men vastly inferior to himself promoted over his head by the politicians in the Continental
Congress and resigned his colonel's commission. He
agreed to head the force to Bennington as a New Hampshire state officer, but not as an officer of the Continental
army.

Seth Warner was at Manchester, some twenty miles
north of Bennington, with the 140 or so survivors of the
Hubbardton battle, waiting for orders. He also had about
200 rangers, many of them Green Mountain Boys, under
command of Col. Samuel Herrick.

Baum's corps marched on August 11 toward Bennington, since Burgoyne had been told that great quantities of
stores had been collected there and were guarded by only
about three or four hundred militia. The Germans
marched south to the Batten Kill River, then through
hilly country to Cambridge, New York, and south to the
Hoosic River.

Ahead of Baum ranged Indians sent with the expedition, who engaged in a wild spree of looting and destruction. When they began killing cows just to get at their
bells, the inhabitants drove the cattle off to safety, depriving Baum of one of Burgoyne's objectives. At Bennington,
Stark heard of these raids and sent out a party that delayed Baum by destroying a bridge in his path.

The German commander took possession of a mill on
the Owl Kill. There his scouts reported that instead of a
mere three or four hundred troops at Bennington, there

were between 1,500 and 1,800. This dismayed Baum not at all; he sent word of it to Burgoyne, adding confidently that these peasants would leave at his approach and "we will fall on the enemy tomorrow early."

The battle of Bennington was fought along the Walloomsac River, at that point a brownish creek flowing slowly in tortuous curves like some long, torpid serpent through rolling country toward its junction with the Hoosic. In this valley, on August 14, Baum's Germans and Stark's Americans sighted each other. Since Baum gave no indication that he was ready to attack, Stark withdrew his army a few miles toward Bennington.

About half a mile west of where a bridge spanned the Walloomsac rose a hill some three hundred feet high. Baum's force occupied the hill, a most advantageous defensive position. The east side, fronting toward the Americans, was steep, with slate ledges that would make storming it a dangerous and difficult operation. But as Stark's scouts soon reported, the north and south slopes were much gentler and covered with trees that would afford good cover in an assault.

In spite of his apparently good position, Baum seems to have become a little worried. That night of the 14th he sent Burgoyne a dispatch asking for reinforcements.

Stark had planned to attack the next morning, August 15, but throughout the day there was a steady downpour that made a battle impossible. Nevertheless, during the storm, Baum was busy placing his troops in the battle formation he had chosen.

Along with one of the 3-pounder cannon, he kept his own 170 dragoons on top of the hill, protected by a wooden breastwork covered with earth. A short distance down the hill British Captain Fraser (his first name, like Burgoyne's Brigadier General Fraser, was also Simon) was stationed with twenty redcoat marksmen, behind a long and earthen breastwork. Still farther down, also protected by a breastwork, were fifty German light infantry.

At the bridge over the Walloomsac, Baum placed his men in some cabins, since he did not want his victorious march into Bennington delayed by a destroyed bridge crossing. In the rear of this guard were fifty German infantry and some Tory soldiers.

Across the Walloomsac, on a knoll, Baum placed 150 Tories, protected by a rather flimsy barricade of fence rails and earth. And behind all these detachments the Indians lurked.

Baum made a mistake in breaking up his army into so many sections. Stark saw at a glance the best way to meet this arrangement of the enemy troops.

The rain still fell in torrents the morning of August 16, 1777, but about noon it stopped and the sun broke through bright and clear. There is an old saying that Vermont has only two seasons: winter and July. But Stark's weather-wise men knew this wasn't going to be a chilly August afternoon. It would be "tarnation hot."

In his camp on the Bennington road, Stark now had about 2,000 men, having been joined by some militia from the surrounding countryside and Massachusetts. The Massachusetts contingent included some Stockbridge Indians, friendly to the rebel cause.

Today, in the museum in Bennington, Vermont, hangs a faded flag which may be the first American flag carried

The original "Arch of Stars" flag, believed to be the first
American flag carried in battle, at Bennington.

on the battlefield. It has thirteen red and white stripes,
but unlike the modern American flag, the stripes at both
top and bottom are white instead of red. The blue field
contains thirteen white stars, eleven of them in an arch
over the numerals "76."

As soon as the rain stopped, Stark sent 200 New Hampshire troops on a long, roundabout circuit to the left of
Baum's hill, while 300 of Colonel Herrick's rangers and
Bennington militia took a similar kind of route to the
right. Two hundred Americans were in readiness to
assault the Tories on the knoll. The rest of the Americans
Stark held back in reserve. As soon as distant musket shots
told them the two circling American forces had sighted
each other, the main army would assault the hill from the
front while the two other forces would attack the easier
slopes toward the rear.

The main American army had advanced so that it was
in full view of Baum's men and deployed for attack. Stark

and Warner, both mounted, cantered up and down along the American lines, encouraging the men. The Germans were already firing their artillery, and since the screech of a cannonball can be terrifying to an inexperienced soldier who realizes it can carry off his head or cut him in two, Stark called out, "Those rascals know I'm an officer; they honor me with a salute!" Laughter rippled up and down the lines, and the timid ones felt better.

Then came the expected distant musket fire from in back of Baum's hill. Stark pulled out his big old stem-winder watch. It was just three o'clock. Then, according to legend, he cried, "There are the redcoats, and they are ours, or this night Molly Stark sleeps a widow!" The only strange thing about the story is that Mrs. Stark's name was Elizabeth.

The Americans then swept forward. The detachment ordered to attack the Tories fell upon them with such fury that the Loyalists fled for their lives, trying to reach the safety of Baum's hilltop. But between the rain and the digging on the hillside for the defense works, the Tories floundered and slid in the mud and many were picked off by the Americans. Then the Canadians guarding the bridge, and troops Baum had stationed nearby were driven off. And the Indians in the rear, once more a thorn in Burgoyne's side, decided they wanted none of such slaughter and flitted away into the forest.

Stark's main body then forded the Walloomsac and began the charge up the hill, while the 500 in the detachments back of it did the same. It took the Americans an hour and a half to reach the summit. The enemy troops part way down fought fiercely and the battle raged so hotly that Stark later wrote: "The firing was like a continued clap of thunder." But for the attacks from the back of the hill it might never have been taken.

The turning point of the assault came when the ammunition wagon containing all of Baum's reserve of powder and ball was somehow ignited and blew up with a roar that made the ground at the summit tremble. The overjoyed Americans then swarmed over the hilltop, yet although Baum's Brunswickers were out of ammunition they clubbed their muskets and drew their great sabers to fight on. But the Germans were trapped from all directions now, and few escaped. A musket ball struck Baum in the stomach and he collapsed.

That seemed to be the end. Resistance on the hill ceased and they carried brave Lieutenant Colonel Baum on a stretcher to a farmhouse, where he died.

The Americans then scattered to round up the prisoners, who were tied to ropes called coffles and marched into Bennington. The wounded were taken there in carts and the dead on the field were collected for burial.

But the battle of Bennington was actually far from over. When Burgoyne received Baum's appeal for reinforcements he had dispatched Lieut. Col. Heinrich Breymann with about 650 Brunswickers—grenadiers and jägers—and two field guns to join Baum. They had marched on the morning of August 15 in the driving rainstorm of that day.

The going was terrible, the road a sticky quagmire, and the German soldiers, especially the grenadiers, cruelly overloaded. Not only were their uniforms heavy, but they were burdened with long, heavy muskets, bullet pouches, powder horns, canteens, knapsacks and sabers so long they almost dragged on the ground. Their legs were encased in leather jack boots coming to their knees—all this topped off by the conical hats that looked like nothing so much as dunce caps with a colored pompon at the peak. Breymann's corps advanced half a mile an hour, and when it halted for the night in the still pouring rain it had marched only eight of the twenty-five miles it had to go.

The next day was just as bad if not worse. All through the morning the rain pelted the water-soaked Germans. The sun came out and beat down ferociously, and the sweating men cursed as they slapped at midges and the little black flies, so small the Indians called them "no-see-ums." It seemed incredible that such a tiny insect could bite so viciously. It was half past four in the afternoon when they reached the mill Baum had seized on his march, with six more miles to go.

Yet Breymann's tired Germans slogged onto the battlefield at the precise moment they were needed. Stark's men were so scattered that he could not reorganize them to meet this unexpected threat to their glorious victory. Burgoyne's gamble on Colonel Skene's advice might have succeeded but for what seemed like a miracle.

At that moment more reinforcements arrived, but these were Americans—Colonel Warner's Green Mountain Boys and other troops who had been summoned from Manchester before the battle began. They too had pushed ahead through the rain all day on August 15 and marched on the next day, stopping at Bennington to dry their muskets, draw dry powder, wet their parched throats with water and whet their courage with a ration of rum.

They charged onto the battlefield to meet the approaching Germans. Meanwhile, Stark collected his men, formed them for battle again and joined Warner's force. Even then, Breymann might have won if his ammunition had not run short. His field guns, 6-pounders, did terrible execution among the Americans. But Stark's army still had powder and bullets. Breymann was forced to order a retreat. He had to abandon his artillery, for the horses were all either exhausted or dead.

At first, Breymann's men were able to withdraw in good order, but the pursuing Americans picked them off in such numbers that some of the Germans broke and ran, throwing away their muskets, while others fell to their knees, begging mercy. Only darkness saved Breymann, himself wounded in the leg, and two-thirds of his force. Stark said, "Had day lasted an hour longer we should have taken the whole body of them."

Burgoyne, writing to Lord Germain after the battle, for once in his military career turned a brilliant phrase that sums up the results of the battle of Bennington. He wrote that the New Hampshire Grants was "a country which abounds in the most active and rebellious race on the continent, and hangs like a gathering storm on my left."

Bennington was the third and last of the mistakes that contributed to Burgoyne's doom. That grandiloquent threat to loose his Indians on the settlers was unwise. Even in the face of his shortages of horses, wagons and food, if he had moved straight from Skenesboro before the road was blocked and before Jane McCrea could be killed, he could have fallen upon Schuyler's wretched little army and won.

And even then, in spite of these mistakes, if Gen. Sir William Howe had come up the Hudson to unite his powerful army with Burgoyne's, the results of the battle might have been different.

11

And Howe, Oh, Where Was He?

WITHIN A FEW DAYS AFTER BURGOYNE AND HIS ARMY reached Fort Edward, Gentleman Johnny had every reason to believe he could crush General Gates' Northern Continental army, in spite of the mistakes he had made. Under the invasion plan, Gen. Sir William Howe, with his huge army in New York City, was to make a "junction" with Burgoyne, either somewhere up the Hudson or at Albany. At that time it was not believed Burgoyne would need Howe's aid before he met the Americans. It has been mentioned that before Burgoyne left London in April, 1777, Lord Germain had promised to write Sir William "by the next packet" about the invasion plan.

But at Fort Edward, in the early part of August, Burgoyne received a letter from Howe in New York dated July 17. It said in part: "My intention is for Pennsylvania, where I expect to meet Washington. . . ." There was no mention of having received a letter from Germain.

Whatever had happened to the letter, Howe and his army could not come to the aid of the now desperate Burgoyne. Nevertheless, Gentleman Johnny went on, even though he had lost over 800 men in killed, wounded and captured at Bennington, more than half of them seasoned regulars. As for the Indians upon whom he had placed such reliance, they held a war council and decided to go home. All but about eighty of the red warriors then left.

Burgoyne's Tories could not be relied upon, either. He wrote Germain that he had only about 400 dependable ones, and half of these had no guns. He certainly could have used St. Leger's force now.

Burgoyne moved his army down the Hudson from Fort Edward to Fort Miller, a few miles above Saratoga. He still clung to the hope that Howe would come to his aid once he was through with Washington in Pennsylvania. If Burgoyne could reach Albany he could fortify the town and wait there for further word from Howe. He still was counting on Howe to carry out the plan in Germain's letter.

Meanwhile, Gates, whose army then numbered about 7,000, was looking for a good place to meet Burgoyne. He finally selected Bemis Heights, near Saratoga, moved the army there September 12, and set up his headquarters.

Bemis Heights was on a bluff rising steeply more than a hundred feet above the Hudson River. North of the bluff a plateau rose even higher, cut by several ravines, the widest and deepest of them being the Great Ravine. The whole area was forested, with a few small clearings.

It was an excellent choice for the American position. And Gates was fortunate in having as his chief engineer

Col. Thaddeus Kosciuszko, an expert Polish officer who had come to America to aid the cause of liberty. It was Kosciuszko who had most strongly advised the pigheaded Gates to fortify Sugar Loaf before Burgoyne reached Ticonderoga.

Kosciuszko fortified Bemis Heights well. The main defensive work was in the form of three sides of a square, with the edge of the bluff making the fourth side. Outworks of logs and earth were also set up and the whole interconnected by trenches. If a retreat became necessary it could be made over a bridge of boats across the Hudson at the foot of the bluff.

At Fort Miller, Burgoyne had to make a choice. He was on the east side of the Hudson, and Albany was on the west at a point where the river was wide, and a crossing would be difficult, especially since the Americans would move down there to block him. On the other hand, if he crossed immediately, there was Gates' camp at Bemis Heights in his way. Burgoyne finally chose to cross at once and meet Gates in a battle.

Since Burgoyne had been reinforced by the coming of 300 regulars from Canada, he now had about 6,000 men. On September 13 this army crossed the river to Saratoga, and on the 15th it marched south in three columns. Because Burgoyne now lacked expert Indian scouts, he did not know exactly where the Americans were until he was within four miles of Gates' camp. Then he made ready to attack.

The first of the two engagements known generally in history as the battle of Saratoga took place on September 19. It was called the battle of Freeman's Farm. Burgoyne's main army took up a position south of the Great

Ravine, with the main American defense work a little more than a mile farther south. However, he sent his right wing of about 2,000 British, Brunswickers, Canadians, Tories and a few of his remaining Indians to make a wide sweep to the right under command of General Fraser. If they could get through they hoped to establish themselves on an elevation to the right of the Americans, an excellent place from which to fire down on them.

About one o'clock that afternoon, Burgoyne believed Fraser's right wing had gained its objective, and under his command the center column of his army marched forward to attack. Unfortunately, Fraser never reached the height he wanted to occupy. A force of sharpshooting Virginia riflemen under the famous Col. Daniel Morgan had sallied out and routed Fraser's men. But a strong force of Tories fell upon Morgan's men with such fury that they too were scattered.

The battle at once became an intense seesaw affair, with the advantage veering back and forth between the American and British forces. Then, on the field, Benedict Arnold detected that Burgoyne's center was weakening. Hoping that with reinforcements he could cut it in two, he galloped headlong back to headquarters and demanded some. Gates, who never stirred from his well-protected headquarters during the battle, refused, afraid to "weaken his lines."

Arnold and Gates, always at odds had a violent argument. At last Gates was persuaded to send out one brigade, but he also ordered Arnold not to return to the battle.

The single brigade of reinforcements was not of course enough to gain a breakthrough in the British center. At last General Riedesel, commanding the British left wing, charged into the thick of the battle with his own regiment and its guns. But for the falling of darkness, Burgoyne might then have won the battle of Freeman's Farm, but the struggle was indecisive. The British suffered by far the most serious losses—about 600 killed, captured or wounded, while the Americans had 65 killed, 218 wounded and 36 missing.

Yet the British now had a fine chance to attack and win the next day. Besides an American shortage of ammunition, the dissension between Gates and Arnold was an even more serious problem. The army itself was divided, with most of the officers favoring Arnold and therefore less willing to use their best efforts to bring glory to a commander they detested.

But that next day, September 20, Burgoyne waited, for no apparent good reason. Certainly his men were in no greater need of rest than the Americans. It was not until the following day, the 21st, that a good reason for still further delay did develop. Burgoyne received a message from Sir Henry Clinton, who had been knighted after seizing Newport, Rhode Island in 1776, and was commanding in New York City during Howe's absence in Pennsylvania. Clinton was coming up the Hudson to attack American Fort Montgomery near Peekskill.

Burgoyne got the idea from the dispatch that Clinton would continue on up the Hudson when he had taken care of the fort. He sent off two couriers, each with the same message to Sir Henry: Send help. Meanwhile, Burgoyne would wait until he had an answer. He could hold out till October 20, he told Clinton.

So Burgoyne's army dug in, entrenched itself on the

battlefield of Freeman's Farm and waited. The delay
was advantageous to the Americans, as hundreds of additional volunteers were flocking into Gates' camp each day,
many influenced by Jane McCrea's murder. And meanwhile the Americans had time to strengthen their
fortifications.

One of Gentleman Johnny's messengers did not get
through and was probably captured, but the second one
did reach Clinton. Sir Henry left New York with a fleet of
warships and transports carrying 4,000 British and German troops. Coming up in Gates' rear, they could have
turned the tide for Burgoyne at Saratoga.

Clinton's force captured Fort Montgomery and its
nearby companion, Fort Clinton (named for an American general, not Sir Henry). Clinton then seems to have
considered going to Burgoyne's aid, though the reply he
sent to Gentleman Johnny's appeal promised little and
merely wished Burgoyne good luck. However, he received a dispatch from Howe in Pennsylvania urgently
demanding reinforcements, and therefore Clinton sailed
back to New York. Burgoyne never got his reply from
Clinton, since the messenger was captured, but on the
day Clinton's reply was written, the worst had already
happened to Gentleman Johnny.

Burgoyne was now in terrible straits. Nevertheless, he
decided to risk everything and strike. When he did so on
October 7, 1777, his crippled army, reduced by desertions
to about 5,000 men, was facing an American force of
11,000, and his food supply was very low.

He held a council of war at which it was decided the
best move would be to probe first at the left side of the
American lines, the most vulnerable to attack. Then, if a

full-sized assault seemed advisable, the rest of Burgoyne's army would join the 1,600 men sent out ahead of it.

It was a gamble in which the odds were strongly against Burgoyne. Yet something had happened in the American camp that came within a hair's breadth of handing the final victory to Gentleman Johnny. Gates and Benedict Arnold had gotten into a bitter quarrel, which resulted in Gates relieving Arnold of all command. Practically all Gates' officers except his chief supporter, Maj. Gen. Benjamin Lincoln, were outraged. They signed a letter urging Arnold to stay in the camp, and Arnold did.

When Gates learned that Burgoyne's advance party was approaching, as usual he hesitated. Then, although he had so many troops available, he sent out only two brigades to meet the enemy. Throughout the battle of Saratoga he seems to have been concerned solely with his own safety, because he kept so many troops in the main fortification on Bemis Heights. Later, however, he did grudgingly send out one more brigade.

Soon after the battle began, the Americans appeared to have complete victory within their grasp. Daniel Morgan's men struck the enemy advance party like a hurricane, his sharpshooting Virginia riflemen mowing down the enemy until they threw away their guns and fled in disorder back to their trenches.

Riedesel, in command of the British army's center, was thus left unsupported to his right. Against him the American brigade commanded by Brig. Gen. Ebenezer Learned advanced cautiously. Then, suddenly, a small man in an American general's uniform, mounted on a bay horse that looked too big for him, galloped out of the Bemis Heights fortification and took over command of

The traitor-to-be, Benedict Arnold, dismissed after a quarrel with Gen. Gates, ignored it by dashing onto the battlefield to become the real hero of Saratoga.

Learned's men. As he swept to the head of the brigade the soldiers gave him a rousing cheer. It was Benedict Arnold, who had defied Gates and come into the battle. As a general and leader, Arnold was incomparable; he had that spark given to few men—the ability to inspire men to do impossible things.

The irate General Gates was beside himself at such insubordination by the man he had dismissed. "He may do some rash thing," he said, and sent an aide in pursuit to order Arnold back, but the officer could not catch him.

Even Arnold's appearance on the field was not enough to overcome the strength of Burgoyne's center. Riedesel's Brunswickers, reinforced by detachments of other Brunswickers and some Hessians, stood fast and repulsed

Arnold's force. But Arnold was far from beaten. The rest of the American army, apparently without orders from Gates, moved onto the field. Arnold led two more brigades in an assault on the British redoubt at the western end of the Great Ravine and then took Learned's brigade into the same attack. Meanwhile, other American units moved in until this redoubt, occupied by Breymann's Brunswickers, was surrounded, and when Breymann himself was mortally wounded, they surrendered.

Now, at last, the aide Gates had sent to order Arnold back to headquarters caught up with him. In the attack on the redoubt, Arnold's horse had been shot dead under him and the thigh bone in his own leg was fractured by a British bullet. Arnold obeyed Gates' order and was borne back to the American camp lying on a stretcher. He had put the Americans in a position to attack Burgoyne's main entrenchments.

Darkness however, ended any chance of overwhelming the rest of the British army. During the night Burgoyne withdrew north of the Great Ravine.

The second and last Saratoga battle, sometimes called the battle of Bemis Heights, sometimes the battle of Stillwater, was over. Burgoyne had lost his last desperate gamble, and it had cost him 600 men killed, wounded and captured, while the Americans had lost only 150.

Burgoyne moved his army back to Saratoga. There, on October 17, he called a council of war. His army was surrounded on three sides by the Americans. He had no boats to escape on the Hudson. The ten cannon he had used in the second battle were lost. So Burgoyne asked for a parley.

On October 17, 1777, he delivered up his sword to

The tide of the Revolution swings toward America as Gen. Burgoyne surrenders his entire army at Saratoga. YALE UNIVERSITY ART GALLERY

Horatio Gates and surrendered his army—a quarter of all the enemy troops in America. The wonder is that Gates, considering his role in the battle, had the gall to stand before the American army and accept the sword as the victor.

As a part of the surrender agreement, the British officers were quartered in Boston for some time before they were sent home to England. There is a legend that when General Burgoyne rode into Boston through streets jammed with jubilant humanity, his arrival was greeted with complete, courteous silence—with one exception. One old crone among the spectators had not forgotten Burgoyne's boast when he arrived in the city in 1775: "What! Ten thousand peasants keep five thousand King's troops shut up? Well, let *us* get in and we'll soon find elbow room!"

And so, the story goes, the old lady cackled: "Make way! Make way! Give the general elbow room!"

Whether Burgoyne heard the words, if they were spoken, is not known, but later he wrote politely to Brig. Gen. William Heath, in command at Boston: "Sir, I am astonished at the civility of your people: for, were you walking the streets of London, in my situation, you would not escape insult."

Although Burgoyne made his mistakes, and some were serious, the great invasion that was his idea should have succeeded. He ought to have won, but for the negligence of Lord George Germain.

Exactly what did happen to Germain's letter to Howe is not definitely known. The letter, outlining the invasion plan, seems to have been written, and General Howe to have received it, but by the time it reached him he was aboard the British fleet with his army, approaching the entrance to Chesapeake Bay. He planned to sail to the head of the bay, land his troops and march for the American capital, Philadelphia, presumably meeting Washington on the way. There has been a good deal of argument among historians about Germain's letter, and as has been mentioned, one respected historian has written a fairly convincing argument defending Germain. But most of the evidence against the British Colonial Secretary is damning.

Howe received the order on August 16, the day of the battle of Bennington. Where had it been since it was written in March? Most historians are convinced that Germain either put it in his pocket and forgot about it for some time, or turned it over to a subordinate who did the same thing. When Burgoyne got back to London he wrote a scorching criticism of Germain for his negligence.

It was not Gentleman Johnny Burgoyne who lost the invasion of America from Canada in 1777. It was Germain, who not only failed to notify Howe in time to help Burgoyne, but failed in his responsibility to see that Burgoyne had all the troops and equipment he had asked for.

Ironically, of course, Gen. Horatio Gates was hailed throughout the colonies for a victory that really belonged to Benedict Arnold. Gates' sense of self-esteem as a result of the battle was to lead to trouble later in the war.

12

Bloody Footprints in the Snow

CONSIDERING THAT SIR WILLIAM HOWE WAS ACTUALLY A brilliant general and fighting man, it is hard to understand why he did not take advantage of the opportunities that could have led to quick victory over the Americans in the Revolution. The most glaring of all the chances he missed came during the winter of 1777–78.

That winter was a time when Howe, like a professional boxer, had his opponent reeling, staggering, hanging on the ropes and wide open for the knockout blow. Simply by marching his army about twenty miles, Howe could have demolished Washington's Continental army.

He did move earlier when he took about 16,000 men aboard the 245 transports and supply ships and the 16 warships that made up the fleet under his brother's command and sailed southward from Sandy Hook on July 23, 1777. He left 7,000 troops to protect New York City.

Washington, in Morristown, New Jersey, learned of Howe's departure the next day, although he did not know

just where the British would land. He had been expecting
they might go up the Hudson to aid Burgoyne and had
made plans to stop them if possible. But if they were
headed south, they might sail up the Delaware River to
Philadelphia, approach the American capital by way of
Chesapeake Bay or head for one of the seaports in the
southern American colonies. Howe could be a tricky man,
and Washington knew he must move south also.

By August 22, intelligence of the British fleet's movements convinced the commander in chief that Howe was
headed for Philadelphia by way of Chesapeake Bay. By
that time he was camped about thirty miles north of
Philadelphia. He moved the army through the city and on
toward the head of Chesapeake Bay. He also sent for Maj.
Gen. John Sullivan, who had been exchanged after his
capture on Long Island, to join him with 3,000 men who
had been left at Morristown.

Howe's fleet reached Head of Elk at the northern end
of Chesapeake Bay on August 25. The troops landed and
advanced slowly toward Philadelphia, looting the prosper-
ous Maryland countryside as they marched. Meanwhile,
Washington had selected Chadd's Ford on Brandywine
Creek, about twenty miles southwest of Philadelphia, for
his stand against Howe.

Sir William proved his ability as a general at the battle
of Brandywine on September 1, 1777. Although Washington had a good battle plan, his intelligence reports were
poor and he learned too late that a maneuver by Howe
had split the American army in two and forced it to
retreat to avoid being surrounded. Howe's success at
Brandywine put him in a position to capture Philadelphia.

Superior generalship enabled Howe to win over Washington's army at the battle of Brandywine. NEW YORK PUBLIC LIBRARY PICTURE COLLECTION

The Continental Congress fled from the city, first to Lancaster and then to York.

Brandywine, though no knockout blow, was a serious defeat for Washington, for somewhere in the neighborhood of 1,400 were killed, wounded and captured, while the British losses were less than half of that. If Howe had moved swiftly he could have taken Philadelphia at once, but for some reason he did not. That gave Washington time to withdraw to his main supply depot to replace his ammunition, most of which had been soaked in a rainstorm.

Meanwhile, Howe captured Philadelphia without a struggle. He left some 3,000 troops in the city under General Cornwallis, who was with Howe's expedition, scattered other British detachments along the Delaware River and then camped with the army's main body of about 8,000 at Germantown, just outside Philadelphia.

Washington had strengthened his army during this

interval to about 8,000 Continentals and 3,000 militia. Since it thus outnumbered the British at Germantown, he decided on a surprise attack by night. The British had camped in battle formation, but had no fortifications, and the chances for an American victory were excellent.

The attack strategy seemed sound. Washington had learned the exact layout of the British camp and made his plans accordingly. He would march on Germantown from the northwest and attack before dawn over a road that divided so that his men could make a three-pronged assault on the camp; at the same time forces under Sullivan and Brig. Gen. John Armstrong would strike from the west. All troops were to attack at the same time.

The various units marched at 7 P.M. on October 3. Everything went well until the guide for Nathanael Greene's left wing got lost in a mist that soon turned into

The thick-walled Chew house, at the right in this drawing, proved the turning point for the British victory over Washington át Germantown. NEW YORK PUBLIC LIBRARY PICTURE COLLECTION

a thick fog, and these troops arrived late. And the Americans, despite the surprise attack, ran into stiff opposition, made worse by the fog and also smoke from haystacks set afire by the British. Once, great disorder was caused when two American units found themselves firing at each other by mistake.

The turning point of the battle came when 120 redcoats occupied a thick-walled, gray stone house owned by Judge Benjamin Chew, a Tory. After barring the doors, they poured a devastating fire down on the Americans from the shattered upper windows. Cannonballs fired by the artillery ordered up by Washington bounced harmlessly off the stout walls of the Chew house, and when British units that had been forced back counterattacked, the Americans had to retreat.

This was another bad defeat for Washington. There were 152 Americans killed—53 of them on the lawn of the Chew house—521 wounded and 400 captured. The British losses were only 4 officers and 66 men killed, 30 officers and 420 men wounded.

Howe was now secure in his possession of Philadelphia except that his sea communications down the Delaware were blocked by two strong American forts and some warships. It took his army and the British naval squadron until late November to overcome fierce American resistance and gain control of the Delaware.

After the battle of Germantown, Washington shifted his crippled army's camps from one point to another near Philadelphia. But with winter approaching he had to find permanent quarters, and he chose Valley Forge.

Today thousands of summer tourists who visit Valley Forge State Park see a pleasant vista of rolling Pennsyl-

vania countryside, beautifully maintained, well marked
and mapped to show important features of where Washington's army spent the winter of 1777–78. There are
exact replicas of the huts the troops built and occupied.
Visitors can peer inside to see what the men's accommo-
dations were like, inspect the remains of redoubts and
outworks and go through Washington's headquarters. But
it takes exhaustive knowledge of the history and a keen
imagination to picture what Valley Forge was really like
during that terrible winter.

Washington's army was in remarkably good shape and
spirits despite the defeats at Brandywine and Germantown. They had not been humiliated and had given the
British a hard time of it during the battles. And they were
well enough equipped and fed.

But on December 19, 1777, when the American army
marched from its camp at Whitemarsh to Valley Forge,
everything had changed. The weather had been bad for
some time, with snow and sleet. The men's clothing,
which was only suitable for summer, was worn out, and
no replacements were available.

The worst shortage was shoes, and a large proportion of
the army was barefooted or close to it. The well-known
story that the soldiers left bloody footprints behind them
in the snow is true. Washington himself wrote that "you
might have trailed the army from White Marsh to Valley
Forge by the blood of their feet."

In December, 1777, the prospect as the soldiers approached their winter home was one of a bleak wilderness,
forbidding and inhospitable, with no shelter. Those who
had tents found no comfort in them on a bitter winter's

night—no fire, no protection from the cold, and thousands of the men had no blankets.

As the snow was falling, they made temporary shelters out of brush covered with leaves. At least there was plenty of firewood, and though it was green and smoked horribly, most of the soldiers spent the night huddled over the thousands of campfires.

Orders for building permanent huts were issued immediately and work on them began the next day. When a tree was felled for firewood, all parts suitable for the huts were set aside. The huts were all alike—sixteen feet long by fourteen wide, the sides and ends of logs, roofs of solid slabs made as tight as possible, and the sides chinked with clay. The side walls were six and a half feet high. At the rear was a wooden fireplace eighteen inches thick; at the front, opening into the company street, a door of slabs if boards could not be obtained. As for beds, parties were sent out to collect from outlying farms the straw left from the threshing of the grain.

Acknowledged as the second greatest American Revolutionary general, Nathanael Greene was at Valley Forge before going south to lead one of the most brilliant and successful retreats in military history.
YALE UNIVERSITY ART GALLERY

A glimpse of the indescribable sufferings of the American army at Valley Forge in 1777–78. NEW YORK PUBLIC LIBRARY PICTURE COLLECTION

Within two days after the army's arrival, provisions were scarce and a cry of, "No meat! No meat!" echoed through the camp. The prescribed day's ration for each man was a pint of milk, a quart of beer, a pound of bread, a pound either of meat or dried fish, and some peas, beans and butter. They actually lived mostly on fire-cake, which was flour mixed with water and, if there was any, a little salt, the whole baked on a griddle, and not a very palatable meal.

Impossible as it is to describe the privations the American army endured, entries in some of the many soldiers' journals give some idea of the hardships and suffering. They speak of snow that grew deeper as time passed, extreme cold, piercing winds, an entire Rhode Island brigade without bread or meat for two days, how few men had more than one shirt, some with only fragments, some with none, of the many men in hospitals and neighboring farmhouses for want of shoes, of soldiers who had to sit all night close to the fire to keep from freezing. A dangerous mutiny, barely suppressed, is mentioned in the journal of one of the soldiers at Valley Forge.

General Greene had been appointed quartermaster general, and both he and Washington made heroic efforts to obtain food, clothing and blankets with little success. Greene reported to Washington: "One-half of our troops are without breeches, shoes and stockings, and some thousands without blankets." Lack of shoes was the worst problem; hides were available when there were cattle to be slaughtered, but there were almost no shoemakers in the camp who could turn them into footwear. And a shortage of fuel was another problem. Every day, parties of men dragging little carts they had made went searching for fuel in a countryside now stripped almost bare.

It was mid-January before the last of the Americans were quartered in huts. Each general had a hut to himself, one for the staff of each brigade, one for all of each regiment's officers down to the rank of major, one for all the lower-ranking officers of each two regiments, while a dozen noncommissioned officers and privates were crammed into each of the others. At least those of the lower ranks had the advantage of each other's body heat in addition to the smoky warmth of the fireplace.

Even when there was a thaw, the mud outside forced the men to stay within the huts as much as possible. The cramped quarters soon became infested with lice and other vermin, and because some of the men refused to go out to the latrines in bitter weather, the huts were foul smelling. The soldiers were given the crude form of inoculation against smallpox then coming into use, but there was no protection against the dread disease of typhus, which was the cause of numerous deaths.

The inability to help his wretched men gnawed at General Washington's heart, and his problems were compounded by what came to be known as the Conway Cabal because Maj. Gen. Thomas Conway was involved in it. Most authoritative modern historians doubt that there was ever such an actual organization among Washington's officers, but rather among some politicians in the Continental Congress. Yet at the time of Valley Forge, some high-ranking officers of the army aided in an attempt to depose Washington and put General Gates in his place. Conway, one of the chief conspirators, was a good general and soldier, but habitually discontented. Another of Washington's enemies was Maj. Gen. Thomas Mifflin, who had been appointed quartermaster general, but completely neglected his duties, pleading ill health, and never came near Valley Forge. His absence was one reason why food, clothing and supplies so seldom reached the camp. Washington finally prevailed upon Nathanael Greene to take over the post. Greene did so reluctantly, out of loyalty to Washington, since it took him temporarily out of the ranks of fighting generals. Before the winter was over he succeeded in remedying many of the evil conditions caused by Mifflin's negligence.

Washington had other staunch friends, including his able chief of ordnance, General Knox, and the young

French nobleman, the Marquis de Lafayette, who had come to America to aid the cause of liberty.

As for Horatio Gates, while he was apparently not a member of the so-called Conway Cabal, he seems to have known all about the plot and done nothing to stop it, although his ill-deserved glory for the victory at Saratoga had obtained him the high post of president of the Board of War. His aide-de-camp, Brig. Gen. James Wilkinson, was deeply involved in the scheme, but luckily for the new nation, these plotters failed in their plan.

Here, then, was the situation of General Washington and the American army at Valley Forge during those frightful winter months of 1777–78. For the first three months, at least, the Americans were in no condition to stand up against the British.

The German officer who joined the American army at Valley Forge in February, 1778, and called himself Baron von Steuben, although he was not a baron at all, was an

At Valley Forge, Gen. Washington prays for the survival of America's cause during the dark days of the winter of 1777–78.
NEW YORK PUBLIC LIBRARY PICTURE COLLECTION

extremely able and experienced officer and a source of
strength to the Americans. He described the situation at
Valley Forge in this way: "The men were literally naked,
some of them in the fullest extent of the word. . . . I saw
officers . . . mounting guard in a sort of dressing gown
made of an old blanket or woollen bed-cover. With regard
to military discipline, I may safely say no such thing
existed. . . . The arms were in a horrible condition, covered with rust, half of them without bayonets, many from
which a single shot could not be fired. . . ."

What was Sir William Howe doing while this American
army, incapable of fighting a battle, was suffering in the
winter gales and snowdrifts of Valley Forge? Why didn't
he march his army over from Philadelphia and wipe the
Americans out? The best answer seems to be that he was
having too good a time, although he was also sick of the
war and had sent his resignation to London a few weeks
after occupying Philadelphia.

Philadelphia, in 1777, was the largest and most important city in America. During Howe's occupation the
population was nearly twenty-four thousand, and bustling
with commercial activity. There were ships, shipyards,
warehouses, iron and flour mills, distilleries, shops, mer-
chants' countinghouses, taverns and clubs. The streets
were paved with brick and many houses were built of the
same material, three stories high. Coaches, chariots,
chaises, wagons and drays clip-clopped and rumbled
along. There was a market nearly half a mile long where
richly dressed ladies came with servants carrying market
baskets.

Philadelphia was different from all the other large
towns in the colonies. It had a hearty, solid air that reeked

of prosperity and good living. And when Howe entered it with his army, the Loyalists among its people gave him a truly royal welcome.

While the American patriots controlled Philadelphia and the Continental Congress sat there as the capital of the new nation, hundreds of wealthy Tories fled to their country estates outside the city, but with the British occupation they came flocking back. A lavish social season began, and nothing was too good for Sir William Howe.

Ordinarily, ladies of high social caste in Philadelphia would have scorned an officer such as Howe, who was, at that time, openly carrying on a notorious romance with Mrs. Joshua Loring, the attractive wife of Sir William's commissary of prisoners. But for Sir William they swallowed their pride and accepted Mrs. Loring. There was an endless round of balls, banquets and receptions.

As for the banquets, Philadelphia was celebrated for its cuisine. While he was there with the Continental Congress, John Adams described the menu at a dinner he attended: "Ducks, hams, chickens, beef, pig, tarts, creams, custards, jellies, fools, trifles, floating islands, beer, porter, wine. . . ." At the home of Chief Justice Chew, whose house in Germantown had been the downfall of Washington's army, John Adams ate: "Turtle and every other thing, flummery, jellies, sweetmeats of twenty sorts, trifles, whipped sillabubs, floating islands, fools, etc., with a dessert of fruits, raisins, almonds, pears, peaches."

Thus Gen. Sir William Howe and his staff dined in Philadelphia, while the starving soldiers at Valley Forge ate their meager rations of flour-and-water fire-cake. Nor did the British officers lack for other entertainment. At the theater in Philadelphia, brilliant, dashing young Capt.

John André, took charge of putting on a number of plays, wrote lines for them and painted scenery. Later André was hanged as a spy for carrying messages between Clinton in New York and Benedict Arnold, about to sell out his country, at West Point.

Besides being in the center of a social whirl, Howe gambled recklessly too. Some of his young officers who could not afford it were his opponents and often they lost; there was criticism of the general for that.

Nor was Mrs. Loring his only feminine companion. Wealthy ladies in Philadelphia were fetching in hoops, furbelows, stomachers, richly embroidered petticoats and capuchin hoods. They carried gold snuffboxes, wore diamonds and had their hair piled a foot or more high on a framework called a *tête*, then much in style. And many handsome young ladies were delighted to dally with the general in command of His British Majesty's troops in Philadelphia.

Of course, the rank and file of Howe's army did not live in such high style. There were some shortages, especially of fuel. But compared to what the American soldiers at Valley Forge went through, the enlisted redcoats and Germans lived like princes.

As spring came to Pennsylvania, things were improving at Valley Forge. More food, clothing and other supplies were coming into the camp. All the huts were up and the place began to look like a neat little military city.

As for Baron von Steuben, he took the army in a firm grasp and set out to make soldiers out of the men once more. He devised a system of drill regulations, and beginning with one small model squad, expanded it to a model company which the officers took turns in handling. He drilled these men for hours, day after day. By late March the whole camp was drilling, discipline had returned, recruits were coming in and the men could take pride in themselves again. The Continental army had survived Valley Forge and was nearly ready to go out and beat the British.

If Gen. Sir William Howe and his friends in Philadelphia gave no thought to their negligence, there was much criticism in England of his failure to annihilate the Americans at Valley Forge. When George III, in the language of royalty, was "graciously pleased" to accept Howe's resignation, there were many who thought Howe should long before have been recalled in disgrace.

But in Philadelphia, when Sir Henry Clinton arrived from New York May 8, 1778, to take command, Sir William was given a farewell party that outdid anything America had ever seen. It was called a *Mischianza*, and Captain André handled the arrangements for it.

It began with a "grand regatta" for the guests in gaily decorated boats on the Delaware. Down river, at the southern end of the city, they landed and walked up a gentle slope between lines of brilliantly uniformed grenadiers at stiff attention, to Walnut Grove, the Wharton estate.

There, seven British officers called the "Knights of the Burning Mountain" jousted with lances in medieval combat with seven others, the "Knights of the Blended Rose," all superbly mounted and attended by esquires. Trumpeters announced the arrival of a herald in black who delivered the challenge to combat. Each knight was the

champion of one of the lovely young lady guests. The
knights charged down upon each other until the chief
marshal announced that all the ladies were satisfied with
their champions' feats of valor.

The four hundred guests then proceeded between two
files of troops and under two arches to the mansion, beautifully decorated for the occasion. There was a sumptuous
supper and a grand ball that lasted until well after dawn.
When General Howe and his brother the admiral entered,
twenty-four slaves in blue and white turbans and sashes
and silver bracelets bowed to the ground as they passed.

On May 24, 1778, Sir William sailed for England. He
remains the mystery man on the British side in the American Revolution. During a public investigation by Parliament after his return, he read an account of his conduct
in America denying that he had failed to do his duty in
any way. His friends managed to have the inquiry
dropped, and Sir William was cleared and went on to be
promoted to a full general.

Yet time after time Howe failed to take advantage of
the chances he had to deal crippling blows to the Americans. Whether each chance was capable of ending the
Revolution is not certain, but there is no denying that if
he had struck during the winter of 1777–78 he could have
destroyed Washington's army at Valley Forge.

13

The British Turn South

NO SOONER HAD SIR HENRY CLINTON TAKEN OVER THE command in Philadelphia than he decided to leave. Ordinarily the capture of an enemy capital often means victory in a war, but Philadelphia was the capital of the new nation only because the Continental Congress sat there, and there was little other governmental organization in the city. When Howe approached Philadelphia, the Congress simply moved to Lancaster and then to York.

The capture of Philadelphia did not mean that the British controlled that region of the colonies. Since Howe had ignored his opportunity to crush Washington's army at Valley Forge, by late spring the new American army was strong enough to lock him into the city with only two routes by which he might escape.

Actually, the British campaign was, like Clinton's ill-fated expedition against Charleston in 1776, a waste of money, men and time. And in 1778 the British were little nearer to subduing the American colonies than they had

Washington leads his army in the grim struggle against Clinton's British army at Monmouth.

been at the start of the war except that they held New York City and Newport, Rhode Island. Meanwhile, on February 6, 1778, France signed an alliance with America. If the British were now to win the Revolution they must act before France had time to supply America with men, money and naval might.

Of the two escape routes Clinton had from Philadelphia, one was to put his troops aboard transports for New York, since he had control of the Delaware River. But the Tories in and around Philadelphia were so terrified of American patriot reprisals when the British evacuated that they flocked into the city, demanding that Clinton take them with him to safety in New York. So many crowded aboard the transports that there was not room enough for the troops to go by water.

The second escape route was to cross the Delaware and retreat across New Jersey to New York. To do this, Clinton faced an almost inevitable meeting with Washington. Nevertheless, Sir Henry decided to march overland.

He did meet Washington at Monmouth Courthouse, New Jersey, on a scorching day in late June that was so hot that out of casualties of about 360 on each side, 40 Americans and 59 British were killed by sunstroke.

The battle was a draw. The Americans would probably have won if General Lee, sent forward with an advance force, had not ordered a cowardly retreat. As it was, the advantage was Clinton's, since he got his army safely to New York. Lee was court-martialed and sentenced first to suspension from his command for a year, but after he wrote an insolent letter to Congress he was dismissed from the American army.

During that summer of 1778, French aid came when Count Charles d'Estaing, admiral of a powerful fleet of sixteen big warships, arrived off Sandy Hook. D'Estaing began his career in the French army, but gained some naval experience and shifted over to the navy. There his record was one failure after another, although he proved himself a brave man. Yet curiously enough, after a most undistinguished naval career, he was commanding a squadron sent to America's aid.

With this mighty French fleet and Washington's army on one side, and Adm. Richard Howe's fleet and Clinton's army on the other, the opposing forces were quite evenly matched. But d'Estaing's ships were so deeply laden that, like Admiral Parker at Charleston, his largest ships could not get across a sandbar at the entrance to New York harbor, making it impossible for the allied forces to try driving the British from New York.

The Americans and French then shifted their attention to New England. The British, having captured Newport in 1776, had that area of Rhode Island under their control. Washington decided to send General Sullivan up there with troops which, backed by d'Estaing's fleet, were to try to recapture Rhode Island. But Sullivan, who was inclined to be hotheaded, got into a quarrel with d'Estaing, and offended the French admiral to such an extent that he refused to take part in the expedition. Nevertheless, Sullivan tried without the much-needed French ships, was soundly beaten and lucky to get his troops out safely.

For the rest of the summer of 1778 there were only a few small battles, since Clinton was preparing for a new and different campaign and had orders to avoid a major engagement around New York. When winter came, Washington took his army back to its old winter quarters in Morristown, New Jersey. Although conditions were not as bad as Valley Forge, there were shortages of clothing, blankets, food and forage that caused a good deal of suffering. There was little action that winter, since battles in that season seldom took place unless there was an especially good reason to fight.

There were some relatively unimportant battles in the north during the summer of 1779, including Brig. Gen. Anthony Wayne's brilliant capture on July 16 of Stony Point, located up the Hudson. From May to September, General Sullivan led a successful and very bloody expedition against the Indians and some British in western New York, and there were a few other minor battles. But the war had reached a stalemate of sorts. While the British still held New York City and Rhode Island, they were far from victory.

However, Clinton's orders, when he took over command of the British army in America from Howe, included a campaign to conquer the southern American states. In November, 1778, he had already sent 3,500 men south by sea, accompanied by a naval squadron, whose first objective was Savannah, Georgia.

Savannah lies fifteen miles above the mouth of the Savannah River. The British transports, guarded by one large man-of-war and three smaller naval vessels, arrived at Tybee Island in the river mouth on December 23, 1778. The commander of the troops, Lieut. Col. Archibald Campbell, was expecting a reinforcement of troops from eastern Florida to join him, but when they did not arrive he decided to go ahead with the assault anyway.

There was a small force of Americans in Georgia, at Fort Sunbury, about thirty miles from Savannah. When their commander, Maj. Gen. Robert Howe (not to be confused with the British general Sir William), learned of the threat to the city he started out with his 700 Continentals and 150 militia to meet the invaders. On the way more militia joined them, bringing their strength to about 1,000 men.

The British flotilla moved up the river to a plantation where the troops landed, and then made their way to the main road to Savannah over a causeway through rice swamps. But on the main road, General Howe had posted an advance force of fifty South Carolina Continentals, who gave the enemy a sharp fire that killed the leader of the

British advance force. Campbell's main body charged the Americans and drove them back to their main force.

Savannah had been fortified some twenty years earlier, but the defenses had now crumbled to ruins. Howe saw it would be useless to try to use them, and stationed his men on the main road over which the British were advancing. He placed two of his three field pieces on the road in the center of his line and the third on his right flank.

The road was a good place for defense, since there were swamps on each side of it, and a trench was dug across the road. But by great good luck Lieutenant Colonel Campbell ran into an aged black man who knew the countryside thoroughly. He guided the British over a little-known road that took them close to the Americans. Campbell then sent his right flank through the swamp in a wide sweep around to the rear of the American right flank. At the same time the rest of his force charged the American lines from the front.

The Americans were caught in a furious crossfire from front and rear. Their center was able to retreat down the road and most of their right flank escaped over a causeway through the swamp, but the left could only flee through a trackless swamp, and in crossing a deep creek many were drowned.

Savannah was now defenseless and fell to the British. The delayed Florida troops then arrived and spread out all over the state. Although the Tories submitted gladly, the American patriots in Georgia had little choice. Soon all of Georgia was under British control, a new royal government was set up and the state was once more a British colony in all respects.

The Americans, however, did not give up hope of recapturing Savannah and eventually the whole of Georgia. The Continental Congress appointed Maj. Gen. Benjamin Lincoln to command the Southern Department, and with a small force of Continentals he went to Charleston, where he learned the British had invaded Georgia. He managed to raise about 1,500 militia from South Carolina as well as some troops which had fled from Georgia. In February, 1779, with new reinforcements, Lincoln began a campaign to dislodge the enemy from Georgia.

One American force of 1,400 North Carolina militia and

At Savannah, Georgia, in 1779, the British besieged and overwhelmed the American defenders of the city.
NEW YORK PUBLIC LIBRARY PICTURE COLLECTION

100 Georgia Continentals crossed the upper reaches of the
Savannah River from South Carolina and took Augusta,
just inside Georgia. But a disastrous British counterattack
routed them, killing nearly 200, most of whom drowned
in crossing a creek, and capturing 173. The rest, having
had their fill of war, just went home. Of the original force
of 1,500 only 450 rejoined Lincoln's army. It was a disheartening blow to the American general.

Nevertheless, new recruits kept joining Lincoln's army.
On April 23, 1779, with 4,000 men, he crossed the river
again to attack Augusta. He left William Moultrie, the
hero of Fort Sullivan's defense in Charleston harbor in
1776, now a brigadier general, on the South Carolina side
with 1,000 men. The British met this move with a counterattack into South Carolina that brought Lincoln hurrying
back there. For the rest of the hot, humid summer of 1779
nothing much happened.

During most of this time, General Lincoln was ill, but
Governor Rutledge and General Moultrie were going
ahead with an ambitious plan. French Admiral d'Estaing
was in the West Indies opposing a British fleet there.
Rutledge and Moultrie sent an urgent appeal for his help
in recapturing Savannah.

On September 8, a powerful French armada arrived at
the mouth of the river. It included two of the biggest warships of the time, ships-of-the-line, each mounting any-
where from sixty to a hundred guns; eleven slightly
smaller and less heavily armed frigates, and nearly a hundred transports carrying over 5,000 French soldiers. The
British commander in Savannah, Maj. Gen. Augustine
Prevost, was warned of the French fleet's approach and

sent an urgent call to Sir Henry Clinton in New York for naval help.

Prevost feverishly began to put Savannah's defenses back in shape, using slaves impressed from nearby plantations in addition to the 2,500 men he had in Savannah. He also recalled 800 British regulars who were occupying Port Royal Island, just off the coast.

Remembering Sir Peter Parker's ill-fated attempt to enter Charleston harbor, Admiral d'Estaing did not try to get into Savannah harbor. He landed the French troops, who made their way slowly toward Savannah, joining the 500-man cavalry force led by Count Casimir Pulaski. Like Baron Kosciuszko this Polish nobleman had also come to fight for America's liberty. Approaching Savannah, they sent a demand to Prevost to surrender.

Prevost badly needed the 800 regulars who had not yet arrived from Port Royal Island. He asked for a twenty-four-hour truce to consider the surrender demand. Foolishly the Americans granted it, inadvertently allowing time for the 800 British reinforcements to arrive. The same day, General Lincoln's force joined d'Estaing and Pulaski, and the following day, when Prevost refused the demand to surrender, the Americans prepared to lay siege to the city.

The start of the siege was delayed because the heavy field guns aboard the French transports had to be landed and hauled over the miry swampland roads. The siege began on September 23 and might have succeeded but for the impatience of the unreliable d'Estaing. He had heard a British fleet was on its way to Savannah, and rather than face it he demanded an assault on the city at once.

On October 9 the Americans and their French allies, with Pulaski's cavalry, launched their attack. They made a courageous attempt, but the British repulsed them all along their lines. Pulaski was mortally wounded, and of the allied attackers, 244 soldiers were killed and 584 wounded. The British defenders lost only 40 killed, 63 wounded and 62 missing.

In spite of the disaster, General Lincoln was not ready to give up, and he continued the siege. But on October 18 the fidgety d'Estaing announced he could wait no longer, the siege was raised, the French squadron sailed away and the Americans withdrew across the Savannah River into South Carolina.

One other British success of some importance took place in the south earlier in that year of 1779. It had no direct result as far as Clinton's campaign to subdue the southern states was concerned, but it was designed to show Virginia what British military and naval might could do and throw a scare into the Virginians that they would not forget. It was a ruthless series of raids that succeeded perfectly and did frighten the settlers along the Virginia coast, but it did not alarm fighting men in the state like Daniel Morgan's Virginia riflemen.

On May 5, 1779, Clinton sent twenty-two transports south from Sandy Hook carrying 1,800 British and Hessian troops commanded by Maj. Gen. Edward Mathew. They were convoyed by a strong naval force. On May 10 they landed at Portsmouth, Virginia, a defenseless town.

From Portsmouth, detachments fanned out through the countryside on and near the coast. They captured small, unfortified towns without opposition except in Gosport.

There a garrison of about a hundred British soldiers burned a nearly completed American warship as well as two French ships loaded with tobacco and other cargo.

But the British raiders also destroyed or captured about 130 vessels and more than 3,000 hogsheads of tobacco in Gosport and other towns. The damage and looting cost the Virginians about 2 million pounds sterling (some 10 million dollars), a prodigious sum in those days, and one which would be a far greater amount today. The invaders then returned to New York without losing a single man.

These raids were not a part of Clinton's main campaign in the south. The subjection of all Virginia was extremely important, Clinton knew, but he was not ready for that yet. He would go after the southernmost colonies first. When he had them back under British control he would take care of Virginia. By late that year the British conquest of the south was well under way, but success was not assured.

14

Clinton's Revenge

SIR HENRY CLINTON WAS STILL SITTING IN NEW YORK WITH about 22,000 men, of whom he had made comparatively little use for many months, but now his southern campaign lay ahead. To strengthen his army he recalled the 3,000 men stationed in Newport, Rhode Island. For three years the British had controlled that part of Rhode Island, but it had added nothing to the prospects of final victory. It was just another waste of military and naval resources, and the only one who profited by it was Clinton, with his knighthood awarded for capturing Newport.

Sir Henry had not forgotten his humiliation at Charleston, South Carolina in 1776. Also, Charleston was important, and the state contained a nest of Tories eager to aid a British invasion. If Clinton could establish a base in Charleston and organize the loyalists as part of his army, he would then be ready to take over South and North Carolina and finally Virginia.

He could easily spare a good-sized force from his huge

army in New York for another expedition against Charleston, especially since Washington's army in the vicinity of New York was not strong enough to attack the city. General Lincoln had only a weak American force at his headquarters in Charleston, and this time the lessons of the 1776 Charleston disaster would not be overlooked.

In December, 1779, Clinton turned over command of the army in New York to the Hessian general, Wilhelm von Knyphausen. On the 26th, Clinton, taking Cornwallis as his second in command, sailed for Charleston with ninety transports loaded with 8,500 of his best troops. They included eight British and five Hessian regiments, five corps of Tories, artillery and cavalry. Five great ships-of-the-line and nine frigates, mounting 650 guns in all, convoyed the expedition.

Clinton had a difficult time reaching Charleston. Off treacherous Cape Hatteras a winter storm of terrible violence struck the fleet and scattered the ships in all directions. One of the transports, carrying Hessians, was actually driven all the way across the Atlantic and was wrecked on the English coast of Cornwall. Most of the horses aboard the other transports died, and many supplies were lost.

It was February 10, 1780, before the fleet was reassembled off the coast of the Savannah River. Clinton then headed north for Charleston, but this time he was not foolish enough to go as far as the harbor mouth. Instead, he put his troops ashore on an island thirty miles south of the city, and advanced slowly northward by land. It took him seven weeks to reach the Ashley River, which flows southward into the harbor.

This gave the Americans time to repair the city's defenses, as well as Fort Johnson and Fort Sullivan, now renamed Fort Moultrie, for a siege. Fortifications circling the city were also repaired, and improved with the help of six hundred slaves Governor Rutledge had impressed from nearby plantations.

The army under General Lincoln was also reinforced. He had some 6,000 men, half of them Continentals and half militia, nearly 400 of Pulaski's cavalry, and also a small naval flotilla of six frigates and three sloops of war. However, four of the ships were useless for fighting since their guns had been removed and sunk to form a barrier between the town and Shute's Folly Island, just offshore. The American flotilla was to be used to keep open an escape route northward, if a retreat were necessary, up the Cooper River, also flowing south into the harbor on the opposite side of the city from the Ashley River.

About thirty miles up the Cooper River, Lincoln had stationed Brig. Gen. Isaac Huger with 500 men, including all the cavalry. Thus, it seemed, Lincoln was protected in case Clinton's powerful army, now increased by 10,000 reinforcements summoned from New York, proved too strong and the Americans had to retire.

Clinton proved himself a capable general in this British assault. He sent a force of 650 infantry and cavalry, commanded by Lieut. Col. Banastre Tarleton, to block the Americans' communication route up the Cooper River. Before the British southern campaign was finished, Tarleton's name would become so fearsome that patriot mothers could frighten their unruly children by telling them that Tarleton would get them if they did not behave.

Educated at the University of Liverpool and Oxford, Tarleton had planned to study law, but changed his mind when a commission in the army was offered him in 1775. Soon afterward he volunteered for service in America. Although he was active in several campaigns in the north, he did not distinguish himself until the southern campaign began. Then, at the age of twenty-six, he found his destiny as a leader of cavalry.

When Clinton landed to begin the new Charleston campaign, Tarleton was in command of the 17th Light Dragoons, but since almost all of the horses had perished on the stormy voyage south, Tarleton and his men roved the countryside picking up horses wherever they could, and in one case attacked a detachment of American infantry and cavalry and seized their mounts.

His men wore green coats and thus became known as the Green Dragoons. Tarleton himself was called the Green Dragoon, and because of a vicious streak of cruelty he earned as well the name of "Bloody Tarleton." During the southern campaign he was completely ruthless and at least once killed enemies who had already surrendered.

On April 14 at three in the morning, Tarleton's dragoons and a corps of riflemen struck without warning at Huger's camp up the Cooper River. They butchered five American officers and fifteen privates with their bayonets and captured sixty other men. Huger and the remainder of his force got away through the swamps, but they left behind 142 loaded wagons and 185 horses, 83 of them cavalry mounts. And at a cost of only two men, Tarleton had cut off General Lincoln's escape route from Charleston.

Meanwhile, Clinton had crossed the Ashley River and

In 1780, Sir Henry Clinton avenged his humiliating defeat of 1776 at Charleston, South Carolina, by besieging and capturing the city. NEW YORK PUBLIC LIBRARY PICTURE COLLECTION

the army entrenched itself eighteen hundred yards from the northwest defenses of Charleston. The army began creeping nearer Charleston by the use of parallels. From the main line of trenches, short ones were dug at right angles straight toward the fortifications. From there a new long line of trenches parallel to the old ones were dug and the army would move forward. This maneuver would be repeated, bringing the British closer each time. While this was being done, the fleet sailed into the harbor without opposition. A fierce bombardment began that did much damage to the city, especially by red-hot cannonballs that set buildings afire.

General Lincoln was hopelessly trapped. He held a council of war on April 19 to which Lieut. Gov. Christopher Gadsden was invited. Both he and the Governor's Council strongly opposed giving up. One councilor even threatened that the people would throw open the city gates to the British if the city were not defended. Lincoln yielded to this for two days, but on April 21 he sent a message to Clinton offering to withdraw from the city if his men and baggage were not molested.

Clinton had Lincoln where he wanted him and knew it. He curtly refused the American proposal, but did agree to a truce to discuss terms. Lincoln demanded that his militia must not be held as prisoners of war and that his surrendered Continentals should march out with the full honors of war. This Clinton also refused, and a terrific bombardment began again on May 9.

The Americans gave the British as good as they sent; nearly 200 cannon were fired at once at the enemy, but with little result, while the British bombardment set more houses on fire. It took just one night of terror and raging fires to make the citizens of Charleston petition for a surrender, to which Lincoln then agreed. His 2,000 Continentals were made prisoners of war, but the militia were allowed to go home as prisoners of war on parole, on the condition that they would not fight against the British during the remainder of the war. Clinton also captured 391 cannon, 5,900 muskets, 33,000 rounds of ammunition and over 8,000 cannonballs, 376 barrels of powder, all American ships still afloat and a tremendous store of supplies.

Losses on both sides, however, were fairly equal. The British had 76 men killed and 189 wounded; the Americans had 100 killed and 150 wounded. This was one of the worst defeats the Americans had suffered during the entire war, and Sir Henry Clinton had his revenge for his failure to take Charleston in 1776. America's chances of winning the Revolution seemed at their lowest ebb, but would become worse in the south.

Clinton then sent General Cornwallis out to subdue the rest of South Carolina. The main post was at Camden in the north central part of the state. An American force of about 350 Virginia Continentals and a few cavalry there retreated toward North Carolina upon the approach of the British. At Camden the British stationed about 2,500 men—regulars, several Tory corps, Tarleton's Green Dragoons and a detachment of artillery.

Tarleton wasted no time at Camden. With his dragoons and some mounted infantry he set out in pursuit of the fleeing Americans under Col. Abraham Buford. He caught up with them on May 29, 1780, in pleasant, rolling farmlands, a region known as the Waxhaws, near the North Carolina border. Tarleton demanded surrender, but Buford paid no attention and kept on heading north. Tarleton's men then charged in on Buford's rear guard. The Americans tried to put up a stiff defense, but waited too long to fire their first volley at the dragoons bearing down on them. Buford's force was surrounded on all sides and surrendered.

Tarleton's cruelty then showed itself in what became known as the "Massacre of the Waxhaws." On the flimsy excuse that some of the Americans had fired after surrendering, he turned his men on them and butchered all but a few. They killed 113 on the field and of the 203 others badly wounded and captured, at least half died later.

Tarleton reported that 5 of his men were killed and 12 wounded.

These senseless murders at the Waxhaws had an effect similar to that caused by the scalping of Jane McCrea at Fort Edward in the north. Although the settlers in South and North Carolina lived in terror of the Green Dragoon, their determination to have revenge was strengthened greatly. The Massacre of the Waxhaws was a British mistake.

Clinton sent out two other expeditions into the interior of South Carolina. One went into the northwestern part of the state and occupied a stockade along an old communication road with the Indian tribes in the west, called Ninety-Six. The other force occupied the region along the southwestern border near Augusta, Georgia. Additional British detachments took other towns until South Carolina was under full British control.

Clinton was satisfied that the conquest of South Carolina was permanent. On June 5, 1780, he sailed back to New York, leaving Cornwallis with 8,000 troops, about half British regulars and half Tory corps. Cornwallis now planned to subdue North Carolina, then Virginia, and thereby end the war.

15

Cowardice at Camden

GENERAL WASHINGTON WAS DETERMINED THAT CLINTON'S conquest of South Carolina should not be as permanent as the British general believed. After the British occupation of South Carolina, a sort of miniature civil war took place there. There were many clashes between patriot and Tory forces in which the British had no part at all and which had no real effect on their control of South Carolina. If the Americans were to have any chance of dislodging the new British commander, Cornwallis, from the state, a strong army must go in and meet him in battle.

Although he could not spare a large number, Washington did send 1,400 crack Maryland and Delaware troops south—splendid fighting men in spite of their comparatively small numbers. They were placed under the command of Maj. Gen. Baron Jean de Kalb.

De Kalb was much like Steuben. He too was not actually a baron, with no more right to use the aristocratic French *de* before his name than Steuben had to the

German *von* denoting a title. When he first came to America to join the patriot cause, this distinguished-looking man had been contemptuous of American soldiers as well as Washington himself. He soon changed his mind, and being an intelligent, competent officer, he won Washington's admiration, and became strongly devoted to the commander in chief. No general in the Revolution showed more courage and heroism in battle than de Kalb, right up to the final moment of his life.

It was unfortunate that de Kalb was not in command of the entire American force, with the reinforcements it picked up, when it reached Camden, South Carolina. If he had been, things might have turned out differently.

They marched south through Virginia and into North Carolina, hearing the bad news of Charleston's capture on the way. De Kalb, hoping for reinforcements now that General Lincoln and all his Continentals were prisoners of war, halted near the north-central border of North Carolina. Since few volunteers were obtained there, de Kalb moved on southwestward to Hillsboro on June 21, 1780, and stayed there a week.

Meanwhile, he had met with nothing but discouragement. He had tried desperately to get provisions and transportation equipment from North Carolina's governor, but in vain. There was a large force of North Carolina militia available, but for the time being, at least, its commander preferred to go his own way, clearing out nests of Tories. De Kalb's men foraged the countryside, but since it was not yet time for the new harvest, supplies of corn were scanty. They reached Deep Run, farther southwest, with no food at all.

Somehow they managed to keep alive during the two weeks they were at Deep Run, living mostly on green apples and peaches, which gave the men indigestion and some the more serious disease of dysencery. A hundred Virginians were supposed to join them there, but they never showed up. De Kalb felt relieved when, after moving on to Deep River, he learned that the Continental Congress had appointed Horatio Gates to head the Southern Department and that the new commander was on his way south. For a competent general like de Kalb, the prospect of leading such a weak army could only be disheartening.

Washington had wanted to send capable Nathanael Greene, and it might have saved the Americans untold trouble if Greene had come then. But in spite of his notorious connection with the now-exposed Conway Cabal, Gates had powerful friends among politicians in the Congress who had sought Washington's downfall. So the commander in chief's choice was overruled. It was one of the worst mistakes the Continental Congress ever made.

Gates was at his plantation in Virginia when the news of his appointment arrived. Nearby lived the disgraced former Maj. Gen. Charles Lee, a friend of Gates. Lee, who in spite of his faults had military ability, warned his neighbor: "Take care lest your northern laurels turn to southern willows," the willow tree being weak and its wood soft. But the jubilant Gates paid no heed.

De Kalb was still at Deep River when Gates arrived with much pomp and ceremony, including a thirteen-gun salute to the new southern commander. Gates allowed de Kalb to keep command of the division he had marched south. The whole force, including expected reinforcements, was to be, in Gates' own words, the "grand army." But it was anything but grand as far as size and equipment were concerned although it was soon increased by Pulaski's former command of sixty cavalry and sixty infantry under Col. Charles Armand, and three small companies of artillery.

De Kalb had planned to approach Camden by a circuitous route through friendly country where supplies and provisions might be obtained. But Gates disagreed and ordered the army to march straight for Camden. The way led through swamps and across many streams that would become raging torrents after a few hours of rain, and also a region so infested with Tories that it was the most unfriendly to the American cause in the entire south.

De Kalb persuaded Otho Williams, a highly competent officer, to try and change Gates' mind. The commander promised to call a council to discuss the matter, but for some reason he never did.

The march to Camden was a terrible one. Food was scarce and the men lived on what corn and peaches they could steal. The farmers of the region fled before the advancing Americans, taking every bit of food they could carry. In an effort to encourage his men, Gates told them a wagon train loaded with food was on its way, although he knew no such thing, and the train never arrived.

Occasionally a stray cow, usually little more than a bag of bones, would provide a scanty meal. On the banks of the Pee Dee River the soldiers were cheered by the sight of cornfields whose stalks were heavy with ears, which they seized and ate ravenously. But it was unripe, and indigestion and dysentery set in.

After crossing the Pee Dee, the "grand army" was reinforced by a hundred Virginia militia. But by that time the other soldiers were enraged at Gates for the decision that had put them through such misery. Only the efforts of the officers, who showed the soldiers their own empty canteens and haversacks, averted a serious mutiny.

At last Maj. Gen. Richard Caswell, who had earlier refused de Kalb's appeal to bring in his North Carolina militia, did come in with 2,100 men. And as the troops approached Camden, 700 more Virginia militia joined Gates. But then Gates yielded to a demand for 400 troops by Brig. Gen. Thomas Sumter, leader of a roving band of South Carolina volunteers, who harassed bands of Tories and the British wherever they could. Sumter wanted to attack a British wagon train, and so Gates sent 100 of his precious Maryland Continentals, some artillery with two field guns and 300 North Carolina militia.

The British garrison at Camden was commanded by Col. Lord Francis Rawdon, but as soon as Cornwallis, who was at Charleston, learned of the American expedition he hurried to Camden. The British strength there was about 2,200 when the battle of Camden began. Gates, aided by still more reinforcements, now had a larger army—about 4,100 men, although only some 3,000 were fit for duty. However, Gates had only the 900 Maryland and Delaware Continentals, while the British had 1,400 regulars.

Gates summoned a council of his officers and read them orders for a night march to Sanders Creek, about seven miles from Camden. The officers were stunned that he would make a move so close to the enemy with a force composed of so many raw militia. However, Gates asked no advice, made it plain that he wanted none, and the officers dared not question this domineering general's wisdom.

At the meeting, Gates gave his officers the impression that he thought his strength was 7,000 men. Otho Williams, who was deputy adjutant general did not believe this count, and he ordered the regimental officers to report how many men they had fit to fight. The colonel showed the total of 3,052 to Gates.

"Sir," said Gates arrogantly, "there are enough for our purpose." Williams knew he could not change the mulish general's mind, so he said no more.

The march began at 10 P.M. August 15, 1780. Gates put the cavalry at the head of the column. Colonel Armand, who was in command of the cavalry, protested, saying the sound of the horses' hoofs would alert the enemy before the main force could come up. Gates pompously dismissed the objection. There is a legend that Gates said, "I will breakfast tomorrow in Camden with Lord Cornwallis at my table." Whether or not the legend is true, it points up the arrogance of Gates.

As was usual, the men were served a ration of meat and corn bread before marching. But instead of the drink of rum issued before a hard march, Gates gave them a gill of molasses. Between the sticky, sweet molasses, the meat that was only half-cooked and the corn bread, which was half-baked, most of the men had severe indigestion on the march, making them unfit for a hard battle.

Through a sultry, airless, moonless night, the half-sick men plodded ahead over a road that was deep sand except where it was boggy when it passed through the swamps.

By a strange coincidence, Cornwallis had also had the idea of surprising the enemy in a night attack and had marched with Colonel Rawdon out of Camden at exactly the same time as Gates's force had begun its journey. At two in the morning of August 16, 1780, the advance forces of both sides met without warning. At first Tarleton's Green Dragoons, charging Armand's cavalry, threw them into scattered flight. But the troops on both the right and left flanks of the American advance closed in and gave Tarleton's cavalry such a storm of fire that they fell back.

The whole engagement lasted only about fifteen minutes. Neither side wanted to continue shooting at targets they could scarcely see in the darkness. The British withdrew to a distance of about six hundred yards.

The Americans held a council, and for the first time Gates' arrogance was missing. Instead of giving orders no one dared question, he asked the officers what they thought should be done. De Kalb and most of the others believed a retreat should be ordered. But Brig. Gen. Edward Stevens of the Virginia militia, who was inclined to be rash, spoke up: "We must fight!" he cried. "It is now too late to retreat. We can do nothing else."

And Gates, in the face of wiser counsel, accepted this advice. "We must fight, then," he said. "To your commands, gentlemen."

Before dawn the American lines were formed. On the right, under de Kalb, were one Delaware and three Maryland Continental regiments, in the center were North Carolina militia, with the artillery in front of them, and on the left were deployed Stevens' Virginia militia, along with Armand's cavalry. A Continental Maryland regiment was held in reserve to the rear.

The British defenses on the left, facing de Kalb and commanded by Rawdon, consisted of Tory infantry. On their right wing were about 1,000 regulars, with two battalions of regulars and about 150 of Tarleton's dragoons stationed in the center to the rear as a reserve. Behind the front line were two battalions of regulars and the Green Dragoons. The British had two 6-pounder and two 3-pounder field guns in front of the center.

The battlefield was a rather narrow area, with pine trees scattered thinly through it. However, in back of the Americans, the dry land between the swamplands on each side was wider. Thus if the Americans had to retreat it would give the British an opportunity to get around their flanks and surround them. On the other hand, the British would be at a disadvantage if they had to retreat, since a wide creek blocked their withdrawal to the rear.

The British did not deploy into battle formation until their column advanced toward the Americans at dawn. When they were less than two hundred yards away, Colonel Williams ordered the American artillery to open fire. As the British deployed into line, their field guns also began firing.

Otho Williams saw a chance for the American left to attack before the British had fully deployed, and he galloped back to suggest it. "Sir, that's right," said Gates. "Let it be done."

Unfortunately, Stevens, on the American left, did not move his militia fast enough to seize this advantage. Williams quickly assembled about fifty volunteers to follow him in a dash to carry out the maneuver. But it was too late and they had to fall back.

Cornwallis had seen the slow, faltering advance of

Stevens' unseasoned militia and he took the opportunity for a charge. Two British regiments, bayonets fixed, stormed down on the Virginians, yelling like demons. Before that scarlet-clad wall of steel, the militia threw away their muskets and ran.

The North Carolina militia in the center saw the Virginians' flight and they too took fright, threw away their guns and fled. The retreating troops charged through the Maryland Continentals in reserve behind the front line and threw them into confusion.

De Kalb managed to reorganize the Maryland men and bring them up to his own right wing, the only remaining force of Americans on the field. This remnant of the army pushed forward and fought a savage but hopeless contest with the now overwhelmingly superior British. The enemy finally opened a hole between the two Maryland brigades and one was routed from the field.

De Kalb was unaware that the other American troops had retreated. It was a hazy morning, and with the smoke from muskets and cannon and the dust kicked up by the trampling feet of the horses and soldiers, it was impossible to see more than a few yards. If de Kalb had realized his tenuous position, he would very properly have ordered a retreat to save his men's lives.

As it was, the remaining Maryland brigade and the Delaware regiment, about 600 men altogether, accomplished an unbelievable feat in standing off 1,000 British regulars and even succeeded at times in driving them back. But the enemy rallied and de Kalb's men were forced to retire, where they re-formed, charged the British again, were again repulsed and then charged a third time.

At the battle of Camden, South Carolina, Gen. Gates sent American hopes of winning the Revolution to their lowest ebb by his incompetence and cowardice in that British victory.

They fought the British for an hour. De Kalb's horse was shot dead, but this valiant man continued to direct his men on foot. A saber stroke slashed open his head, but still not knowing the rest of the American army was routed, he refused to order a retreat. It was bitter, man-to-man, hand-to-hand fighting in this last encounter and for the Americans it was hopeless. Cornwallis threw his entire force of over 1500 men on these brave 600.

De Kalb ordered a bayonet charge, and the Americans surged forward, charging through the enemy's ranks and then turning back on them from the rear. Eleven British bullets crashed into de Kalb's body, and he was mortally wounded, but before he fell he cut down a British soldier about to thrust a bayonet into his breast. At last, with

Lord Cornwallis let Gen. Greene
and his American army lure him into
pursuing Greene's retreat through
South and North Carolina, resulting
in Cornwallis' surrender at Yorktown
and the final American victory in
the Revolution.
NEW YORK PUBLIC LIBRARY PICTURE COLLECTION

their leader dead, the Maryland and Delaware men broke
ranks and fled.

The American defeat at Charleston had been a terrible
one, but this was worse. The survivors were scattered in
all directions for miles. Many were captured by Tarleton
and other pursuing British detachments. The Americans
lost twenty ammunition wagons and all their baggage,
supplies and equipment. It seemed impossible that any of
these troops could be collected to fight again.

Probably about 600 Americans were killed and 1,000,
including the wounded, were captured. Seventy-nine British were killed and 245 wounded, according to Banastre
Tarleton, who wrote a book about the southern campaign.

During the battle nothing more was heard of General
Gates. Most reports have it that he was "swept off the
field" by the fleeing center of the American army. Swept
away he may have been, but he was mounted on a horse
believed to be the fastest in the army. He must have let
this racehorse have his head, for Gates did not stop until
he reached Charlotte, North Carolina, 60 miles from
Camden, where he stayed overnight and then coursed on

until he reached Hillsboro, North Carolina, 180 miles from the battlefield.

Alexander Hamilton wrote sarcastically of this cowardly flight: "One hundred and eighty miles in three days and a half. It does admirable credit to the activity of a man at this time of life." The "great hero" of Saratoga, who had let Arnold and Morgan win his glory for him, the man who had done nothing to stop the plot to depose Washington and put him, Gates, in chief command, had at last shown his true colors.

Cornwallis, taking up where Clinton had left off, now had all South Carolina at his mercy. The American army in the south was a shattered ruin. Before Cornwallis lay North Carolina, then Virginia, which seemed victories easily within his grasp. All he had to do was to strike quickly before the Americans could obtain enough reinforcements from the north to stop him.

16

A Pale Dawn Glimmers

THE SOUTHERN CONTINGENT OF THE AMERICAN ARMY AFTER the catastrophe at Camden was rendered pretty impotent, with troops having suffered heavy losses and been dispersed throughout the countryside. The men had been given no orders before the battle as to where they should assemble in case of defeat. Almost none of the terrified militia came back, anyhow, but about 700 of the surviving Continentals managed to find Gates at Hillsboro. They were in a pitiable condition, hungry, exhausted and almost naked, many without guns.

Gates did at least try to reorganize what was left of his "grand army," but he could only wait and see how many would return and if possible obtain food, clothing, blankets and arms for them.

Although the American force in the South was fairly decimated, Col. Francis Marion was making life miserable for the British in South Carolina. Marion was the American counterpart of Banastre Tarleton, but lacked the Green Dragoon's vicious cruelty. He was a scourge to the British, always turning up with his band of volunteers when least expected, and causing the British untold trouble, loss of men, equipment and supplies by his daring raids.

Marion knew how to maneuver through every inch of the vast South Carolina swamps so well that he was called the "Swamp Fox." The harassed British hounds could not track him down. Like Ethan Allen and his Green Mountain Boys, the Swamp Fox and his men share a certain similarity to the fabled Robin Hood and his merry men of Sherwood Forest.

Despite enemy superiority in numbers Francis Marion was never intimidated. Four days after the battle of Camden, the Swamp Fox with just sixteen of his men swooped down at dawn on a detachment of British and Tories taking 160 American prisoners to Charleston. In a trice Marion had captured the startled enemy and released their prisoners. Unfortunately, less than half of the freed Americans, remembering too clearly the nightmare of Camden, returned to the army.

Marion was a small but mighty pillar for the American cause in the south. About all he could do to help the stricken American army now, however, was to make himself an infernal nuisance to the British. In this sort of warfare the Americans were also aided by two other leaders of volunteer bands, usually called partisans—Andrew Pickens and Thomas Sumter.

As was mentioned earlier, Gates made a mistake in judgment and weakened his army by sending 100 Continentals and 300 militia to reinforce Sumter's band of 300 partisans who planned to attack a British wagon train. For a time it looked as though Sumter might accomplish his design.

On the day before Camden, Sumter attacked the wagon train, capturing 100 British regulars, 50 Tory militia and 40 wagons loaded with stores. But after Sumter had retreated up the Wateree River to a point where he thought he was safe from enemy reprisal, Banastre Tarleton, rounding up Americans fleeing after Camden, spotted Sumter's camp. It was noon; some of Sumter's men were bathing in the river and others sleeping. Sumter himself was sleeping under a wagon. The Green Dragoons slew 150 Americans and captured over 300, releasing Sumter's prisoners and retaking the supply wagons. Although Sumter managed to escape, the chance of success was lost.

Since Cornwallis waited three weeks before leaving Camden, the wretched American rabble of 700 still in North Carolina did have that time to reorganize and recover as best they could. Supposedly Cornwallis delayed to be sure his outposts in South Carolina were safe from attack before advancing into North Carolina. This is difficult to understand, since the only threats to the outposts, Marion, Sumter and Pickens, were still on the loose when Cornwallis did march. At the same time he knew the American southern command had been smashed to such a degree that it could hardly be dangerous, and the survivors had retreated far into North Carolina.

Cornwallis finally began his northward march on September 8. Moving slowly, he reached the scene of the Massacre of the Waxhaws and rested a few days. But beyond the left flank of his advance force, British Maj.

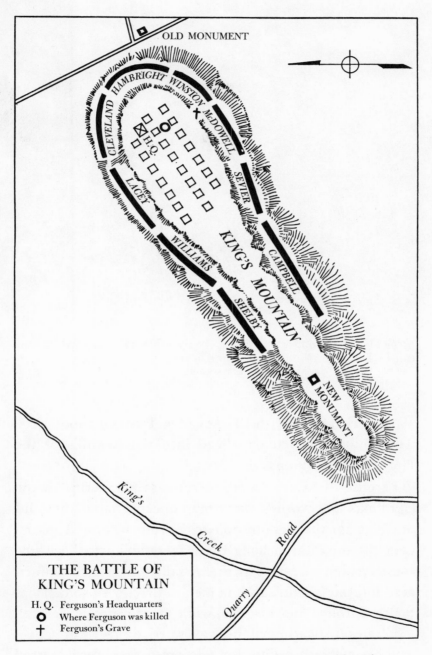

OLD MONUMENT

CLEVELAND HAMBRIGHT WINSTON McDOWELL

H.Q.

SEVIER

LACEY

KING'S MOUNTAIN

CAMPBELL

WILLIAMS

SHELBY

NEW MONUMENT

King's

Creek

Road

Quarry

THE BATTLE OF
KING'S MOUNTAIN

H.Q.   Ferguson's Headquarters
O   Where Ferguson was killed
✝   Ferguson's Grave

An American attack from all directions up the steep sides of
Kings Mountain, South Carolina, proved the undoing of the
British force stationed on its summit in 1780.

Some idea of the difficulties facing the Americans at Kings Mountain can be had from this sketch of the assault on the summit.

Patrick Ferguson, with 100 Tory regulars and about 1,100 Tory militia moved on ahead into the foothills of the North Carolina mountains.

Ferguson had done a lot of ruthless plundering in the Carolinas and warned the mountaineers that if they did not give up their opposition to Britain he would march over the mountains, hang the leaders and lay the whole countryside to waste. His threat rallied over 1,200 infuriated militia, North Carolina men mostly, with some from South Carolina and Virginia, while more were on the way.

Ferguson, hearing of it, was worried. He sent Cornwallis a message asking for reinforcements, then started south for the security of the British-held Ninety-Six outpost. The Americans, led by Col. William Campbell, were hot on Ferguson's trail. They decided to send 900 picked men ahead to catch him.

On October 6, Ferguson's scouts reported the Americans were very close. The British commander was near Kings Mountain, actually a hill about 600 feet high, with a flat top about 500 yards long and 120 feet across at its widest part. The sides were steep and rocky, and it looked like an ideal place from which to repel an attack. Ferguson took his men to the top.

October 7, 1780, dawned in a drizzle, with mists swirling around Kings Mountain. The vengeful Americans reached the mountain about noon and encircled it. Trying to scale those rocky cliffs might seem more foolhardy than the British assault on Bunker Hill, but these were mountaineers as mad as a stirred-up hive of hornets, and the sides of the hill offered them shelter because they were thickly wooded.

Thus protected, the Americans clambered to within a hundred feet of the summit. Up there, on the edge, the Tories had no protection at all, and the mountaineers were crack shots. For an hour they fought, with the Tories taking such severe losses that the Americans were able to work their way up the mountain.

As one American detachment reached the top, Ferguson ordered a bayonet charge that drove them back. But his enemies were swarming up on all sides; as soon as the Tories drove one group back another came at them from a different direction. When an American bullet blasted Ferguson from his horse, the Tories surrendered. One hundred fifty-seven British were killed and 163 badly wounded, while another 698 were captured, many of whom were badly hurt. Thirty prisoners were tried for atrocities previously committed on the inhabitants and nine were hanged.

Military men and historians are generally agreed that Kings Mountain was a bad blunder by Cornwallis and Ferguson. Ferguson and his men got too far away from the main army to obtain reinforcements quickly, and Cornwallis should have realized it. Also, a strategic mistake that was worse was Ferguson's failure to throw up earthworks or some other protection on the edges of the Kings Mountain summit that would probably have pre-

Maj. Patrick Ferguson, commanding the British atop Kings Mountain, was shot and killed as the victorious Americans reached the steep-sided summit. NEW YORK PUBLIC LIBRARY PICTURE COLLECTION

vented the Americans from reaching the top.

For the Americans, the victory at Kings Mountain raised the morale of what was left of Gates' "grand army," which had sunk so low that Cornwallis, as has been said, might easily have finished it off by swift action. At this point, Gen. Nathanael Greene arrived to take command of the wreck that had been an army before Camden.

The catastrophe had taught the Continental Congress a lesson. On October 5, 1780, it passed a resolution saying, ". . . that the Commander in Chief be and is hereby directed to appoint an officer to command the southern army, in the room of General Gates."

Greene was then in command of the fort at West Point. Washington lost not a moment in writing him, ordering that he go south and take over the command. Perhaps no American general ever received an appointment that offered such a small chance of success. In fact, although Greene knew the southern army's situation was critical, he did not know just how bad it was until he reached Gates and the miserable survivors at Charlotte, North Carolina on December 2, 1780.

Washington had ordered Greene to make a thorough investigation and report of Gates' behavior at Camden. At its start the meeting between the two men could only have been a tense one. Not only had Gates done all he could to discredit Washington, but Nathanael Greene, the commander in chief's favorite general, had also felt the full force of Gates' spite.

Thus Gates, of course, was greatly worried. Here was a man he had treated badly and who had now come to relieve him and get the facts about Camden. Yet Greene did all in his power to put Gates at ease and show that he bore no ill will toward the discredited general. Gates never forgot Greene's forbearance. He remembered his successor with gratitude and affection the rest of his life.

Greene had no heart for the investigation. He was immensely relieved when he discovered that few of the officers who could give testimony were at the camp. Washington had instructed Greene that if he decided the investigation should not take place at once, it could be postponed. After consulting other officers in the camp, Greene felt that this should be done.

When Greene informed Gates of the decision, the deposed general said with great dignity, "I would prefer to face it now, General Greene, but if that is the decision I will abide by it." And with that he set out for his plantation in Virginia. Washington never held the court of inquiry.

However, before all this happened in Charlotte, Nathanael Greene had to face his most important and disheartening problem of somehow building a new southern army. On his way south he had stopped in Philadelphia to plead with Congress for men, money, clothing and equipment. He did the same with state officials in Maryland and Virginia. Promises were made but few were carried out.

On his journey south Greene had with him the man who had changed the starving, naked rabble at Valley Forge into a fighting army—Steuben. Greene left Steuben in Richmond, Virginia, to do what he could to raise men, train them and obtain the supplies that were so badly needed. Greene also had Kosciuszko with him in the south, where the Polish general's engineering skill was to be invaluable, as well as Daniel Morgan, who with his Virginia riflemen was soon to save the American southern army from what could have been the final disaster for the Americans.

These three men, the three partisan leaders, Marion, Sumter and Pickens, as well as Col. Henry Lee, more famous as "Light Horse Harry Lee," who joined the southern army in January, 1781, with his Virginia men, formed about the only crutches Greene had to lean on. Greene now had at Charlotte about 1,480 men fit for duty out of more than 2,400 soldiers, only 950 of them Continentals. Less than 800, sick and well, had proper equipment and clothing, and provisions were very scarce.

To meet Cornwallis in battle with such a miserable force would have been suicidal. The British general, meanwhile, was "resting" at Winnsboro, South Carolina, with about 2,000 men. His excuse for not moving was that he was waiting for reinforcements from Maj. Gen. Alexander Leslie, who had been making raids in Virginia.

By waiting for Leslie, Cornwallis gave Nathanael Greene the precious time he needed most of all. The British commander might have marched the seventy or so miles from Winnsboro to Charlotte and annihilated the skeleton of an American army there. Meanwhile, Greene was trying with all possible speed and energy to equip, supply and reinforce.

Greene then made a momentous decision. He divided his army into two parts. The larger portion, about 1,000 men in a division commanded by Brigadier General Huger, moved down to a camp just over the South Carolina border on the Pee Dee River at Cheraw Hill. It was a pleasanter location and in friendlier country than Charlotte. The other part of the force, about 600 men under Daniel Morgan, moved into western South Carolina.

It was a risky business, dividing this army which could hardly be called an army, and against good military practice, but Greene felt it had to be done. He was watching Cornwallis, and under the plan, Cornwallis would have American forces on each side of him. If he marched toward the Cheraw camp the Americans could move eastward, threatening Charleston. If he moved west after Morgan, Huger's force could attack his posts at Ninety-Six and Augusta.

If Greene's strategy worked, the Americans would have Cornwallis in trouble; if it did not, Greene's divided forces could be destroyed, especially if the British reinforcements under Leslie arrived at Winnsboro to join Cornwallis. It was a long chance, but Greene felt he had to take it.

Through the country between Huger's and Cornwallis' camps flowed two large rivers, the Catawba in the west and the Yadkin farther east, both running approximately southward. To move into Virginia, Cornwallis would have to cross the Dan River, meandering eastward back and forth across the North Carolina–Virginia border. Greene intended to use these three rivers to stop Cornwallis if possible.

General Kosciuszko was sent to the Yadkin and Catawba, and his quartermaster, Col. Edward Carrington, to the Dan. They were to explore and map them, showing the location of roads leading to them, of fords and ferries, and also to collect flatboats, some of which

Greene intended to carry with him on wheels or wagons when he moved to head off Cornwallis. The heavy boats would slow his army's progress, but he thought it might prove to be worth it.

Greene was with Huger at the Cheraw base. Daniel Morgan had marched directly from Charlotte with his

How Brig. Gen. Daniel Morgan's American troops were formed to meet the oncoming British under the dreaded Green Dragoon, Lieut. Col. Banastre Tarleton, before Morgan's smashing victory at Cowpens, South Carolina, in 1781.

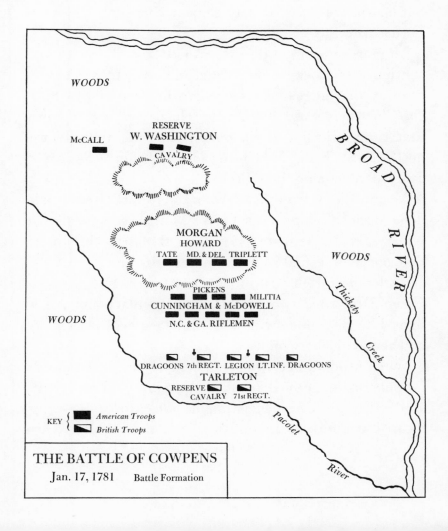

KEY — American Troops / British Troops

THE BATTLE OF COWPENS

Jan. 17, 1781   Battle Formation

force, consisting of his own 200 Virginia riflemen and the other 400, mostly Continentals and some light dragoons. Small as their numbers were, they were mostly crack fighting men.

Morgan was only forty-five, but he had seen years of fighting, first in the French and Indian War, then Pontiac's War in the Great Lakes region and now the Revolution. Exposure to wind and weather, long marches, times of scanty food and clothing, and hard fighting had taken their toll. Morgan was twisted with painful rheumatism, but he was still an extremely dangerous enemy to General Lord Cornwallis.

Morgan moved southwest, crossed the Catawba and continued on, picking up several militia detachments on the way that increased his strength to almost 1,000 men. On Christmas Day, 1780, he reached the Pacolet River that came brawling down out of the mountains to the northwest. There, as Greene ordered him to do, he camped, remaining three weeks.

Meanwhile Cornwallis, aware of what Greene had done, decided he must act before Morgan could strike at Ninety-Six and Augusta. He ordered Banastre Tarleton to take out a force, find Morgan and destroy him.

Tarleton started with about 1,100 men, including his Green Dragoons, two battalions of regulars and a few light dragoons, along with a small detachment of artillery and about 100 Tory militia.

While Morgan had nearly as many men, Tarleton was far superior in trained regulars. Leaving on January 15, 1781, Tarleton headed straight for Morgan's camp, located at a fork on the south side of the Pacolet. When

Morgan's scouts reported Tarleton was coming, he took his force across the river so he could have the stream between him and the enemy. But the Green Dragoon outwitted him by crossing the river six miles downstream. Morgan then withdrew to an area inside a large bend of the Broad River.

The place, a grassy clearing dotted with trees, was called the Cowpens because cattle were assembled there to be driven to market. Military experts call it the worst possible choice of a battlefield because it had no undergrowth to impede Tarleton's horsemen and was a pocket surrounded on three sides by the river bend. But Morgan chose it deliberately, as he later explained, because he wanted to give his militia less chance to flee than they had had at Camden.

17

Cowpens and the Chase toward Ruin

AFFECTIONATELY, HIS MEN CALLED MORGAN "THE OLD Wagoner" because he had begun his military career as a teamster in the French and Indian War. His Virginia sharpshooters respected and loved him, having endured many hardships with him. Now, on the night before the battle of Cowpens, as he walked among them, talking and joking, they were in full respect of him.

He paid special attention to his unreliable militia. He thought if they could stand and give the enemy two volleys their purpose would be accomplished. "Just hold up your heads, boys," he told them, "give them two fires and you're free."

The next morning, after breakfast, Morgan formed his men in an unusual way, for he put his weakest troops, the 300 North and South Carolina militia, in the forefront under Andrew Pickens, who had joined him. If the militia could stand the first shock of combat long enough to fire those two volleys it should give his best troops an advantage at the start. This forward line was thinly spread over about 300 yards. However, still farther in front, Morgan scattered 150 crack riflemen in concealment behind trees. They could help the militia immensely, since the Old Wagoner told the sharpshooters to pick off "the men with the epaulets"—the British officers. They were not to fire until the enemy was within fifty yards.

The main line, behind the militia, contained the all but invincible Maryland and Delaware Continentals in its center, Virginia militiamen and a small company of Georgians on the right, and Virginia riflemen on the left— about 450 men in all. As a reserve in the rear, Morgan placed cavalry—80 mounted dragoons and 45 infantry-men he had mounted and given sabers.

To the jittery front-line militia, Morgan gave orders to fire slowly and deliberately and above all to retire in good order after getting off the two volleys, so as not to upset the troops behind them.

Tarleton, a brilliant officer despite his barbarity, was determined to avenge Kings Mountain and either destroy Morgan's force or drive it back where the advancing Cornwallis could finish it off. He and his men started toward the Cowpens at three in the morning of January 17, 1781.

They stumbled for eight seemingly endless miles over wretched roads that went through swamps and creeks before they sighted the Americans in the dawn. Tarleton and a small advance party, spotted Morgan's badly concealed sharpshooters and the Green Dragoons were ordered forward to rout them out.

The green-coated riders galloped into a tempest of fire

that shot fifteen of them out of their saddles, and the rest turned hurriedly back. The dragoons were shaken badly and could not be induced to charge again, so Tarleton deployed the rest of his troops in battle formation. He put some of his own unmounted men in the center, a regiment of regulars on the left, and his light infantry on the right. A regiment of regulars and 200 cavalry remained to the rear as a reserve. The two 3-pounder cannon, placed one in the center, the other on the left, began firing at once. Then Tarleton ordered the whole line forward.

Pickens' untried militia in the forefront justified every hope of Morgan's. They got off the two volleys with deadly aim, killing more British than fell at any other time in the battle. The enemy line wavered as if it might go to pieces, but it came on once more. This time the American militia retreated toward shelter behind the Continentals on the left. They might not have reached safety if the horsemen of the American reserve had not suddenly appeared to the right of the British pursuing the militiamen. With their sabers drawn, the American calvary charged the enemy and routed them.

The rest of the British army, seeing the American militia in flight, thought it was the whole American line, and they rushed forward into a torrent of bullets that flung them reeling back. But they rallied and came on again, and for half an hour there was fierce fighting in which neither side gave way.

Tarleton then threw his reserve infantry into the battle, sending them far to the left in an effort to outflank and get behind the American right wing. But Col. John Howard saw what was up and ordered the riflemen and

Continentals on the extreme right to fall back a little, wheel to the right and drive off the attackers. The men misunderstood the order, however, and fell back but did not wheel. Seeing this maneuver, the rest of the American line also fell back.

Tarleton thought he had won the battle, and ordered a charge. But the American cavalry who had been pursuing the enemy they had routed when the militia retreated had now returned to the field. Their commander, Col. William Washington, a distant relative of the commander in chief, saw that the advance of Tarleton's line was ragged.

Washington sent word to Morgan: "They're coming on like a mob. Give them one fire and I'll charge them."

Morgan then ordered the Continentals: "Face about, give them one fire and the day is ours!"

The command was obeyed with deadly effect on the British line. Colonel Howard then shouted: "Give them the bayonet!"

With that, the lionhearted Maryland and Delaware Continentals drove into the now wavering British line and split it apart. Howard offered the enemy quarter if they threw down their arms. Muskets hit the ground with a clatter. Some of the British ran; others stood fast, begging mercy. Some of the Americans wanted to give them "Tarleton's quarter" with their bayonets, but the officers prevented it, though with some difficulty.

The battle in the center was over, but not on the American right, where the British dragoons were still fighting furiously. But again Pickens' militia, of whom Morgan had had such doubts, proved they were no cowards. They fell on the dragoons with such ferocity as to rout them. However, the regulars on the British left were still stubbornly resisting, until the entire American force fell on them and forced them to surrender.

But Tarleton would not give up. He ordered his reserve of dragoons in the rear to charge forward, but they refused to obey, and when Tarleton tried to use his field guns, Washington's cavalry rode down on the British artillerymen. These brave gunners never surrendered, and every one was either killed or seriously wounded.

Now, indeed, the battle of Cowpens was over. The American cavalry pursued Tarleton and the fleeing

Col. William Washington's cavalry turns the advantage to the Americans in the battle with British Lieut. Col. Banastre Tarleton and his Green Dragoons at Cowpens.

NEW YORK PUBLIC LIBRARY PICTURE COLLECTION

remains of his force for some time before giving up the chase. But in a few hours, for it was not yet ten in the morning, Daniel Morgan and his indomitable men had won a stunning victory.

The British losses were heavy. Morgan's order to the riflemen to aim at the men "with the epaulets" had been well obeyed, for out of about 100 enemy killed, 39 were officers. There were 229 British wounded and taken prisoners, as well as 600 more captured unhurt. All but a tenth of Tarleton's force was lost to him, while there were only 12 Americans killed and 60 wounded. Captured also were the 2 field guns, 800 muskets, 35 baggage wagons, 100 dragoon horses and some ammunition.

But Morgan was far from safe. He knew Cornwallis would be after him the moment he learned of Tarleton's disaster. Morgan, before retreating northward with all speed, wrote a hasty but complete report of the battle and sent a courier careering eastward with the news for Greene and Huger at Cheraw.

There was a jubilant celebration when the news reached the main army's camp. Nathanael Greene, overjoyed though he was, worried about Morgan. Even though the Old Wagoner was a great fighting man, and his battle formation against Tarleton had been masterly, he was not skilled in military tactics.

Greene decided to make a dash himself to aid Morgan. He left the main army under Huger's command with orders to cut across to the northwest and meet him and Morgan at Salisbury, North Carolina. Then, accompanied only by a guide, one aide and three mounted militiamen, Greene set out westward on January 28 in a mad gallop for Morgan's camp up on the Catawba River, 125 miles away, and through country overrun with unfriendly Tories.

This was dangerous enough, but Huger's orders were even more difficult. Far south though it was, that region of South Carolina was riddled with ice-cold creeks and rivers that must be crossed. And Huger's men were poorly clothed, some even lacking shoes. Food and blankets were scarce and there were no tents at all. Some days the marching men went without meat and even flour. It rained continually, a cold drizzle that soaked them to the skin. Yet they pushed on with what speed they could muster.

Cornwallis had already moved a short distance north to Turkey Creek, North Carolina. There General Leslie and his reinforcements joined him, bringing the British strength to over 3,000 men. On January 19, two days after Cowpens, Cornwallis began his pursuit of Morgan. Believing the Old Wagoner would head for Ninety-Six and attack it, the British general marched northwestward until he learned that Morgan was headed straight north. At a time when every minute counted, Cornwallis' miscalculation was a delay for the British.

Cornwallis then headed for Ramsour's Mills, where Morgan was reported to be camped. But when he reached there, the Americans had been gone for two days and had already crossed the Catawba River. At Ramsour's Mills, Cornwallis made a decision he would regret the rest of his life, although he felt it was his only course if he were to catch the Americans. Ideally, Cornwallis should have sent light troops dashing ahead to overtake Morgan, but they had been lost at Cowpens, so Cornwallis decided to transform his whole army into light troops.

He therefore destroyed all his baggage except for the wagons he must have to carry the barest amount of food, his ammunition, hospital supplies and four wagons for his sick and wounded. The rest, including all his army's tents, was burned. The transformation took two precious days during which about 250 soldiers, mostly Hessians, deserted, probably anticipating the worst.

During this time, Greene and his escort arrived at Morgan's camp on the Catawba. Morgan advised a retreat to the mountains to the west, but deferring to Greene's superior tactical skill, they continued north, hoping they could outdistance Cornwallis. Greene swiftly sent off an order to Huger to make his junction with Morgan's force as soon as possible and also to call in Light Horse Harry Lee and his cavalry, Lee's Legion, from the southeast.

Cornwallis intended to cross the Catawba at Beattie's Ford, but he was delayed two days by torrential rains which had swollen the river, thus making a crossing impossible. While waiting, Cornwallis devised a plan to outmaneuver Greene. He sent one division to approach Beattie's Ford, but this was a feint. Cornwallis and his main army would cross six miles downstream at Cowan's Ford, outflank Morgan's camp and destroy his force.

The British began their crossing at dawn in a heavy rain. The Americans were only partly deceived by Cornwallis' strategy. Col. William Davidson of the North Carolina militia had men guarding both fords. The British met a hot reception at Cowan's Ford, but it was not enough to drive them back. They floundered ashore and then scat-

tered the militia along the river in all directions, killing
Colonel Davidson during the action. Cornwallis' only real
gain was in getting his army across the Catawba safely,
with few losses, and in depriving Greene of the militia.
Morgan's main column was already thirty miles away.

A rendezvous had been set near Salisbury for the
militia to reassemble in case of defeat. Greene, who had
remained in the rear, waited there until midnight, when
a messenger arrived with the news that Davidson was
dead and the militia in flight. Greene's spirits were at their
lowest ebb during the entire retreat when he realized that
the militia would not return, and he was now almost in
despair over Morgan's chances of escaping.

The great retreat was still on, nevertheless—about
3,000 British chasing some 2,000 Americans in their desperate race for Virginia where they could obtain reinforcements and supplies and make a stand against
Cornwallis. But there remained two more rivers to be
crossed—the Yadkin and the Dan. High water in either
one might force one army or the other to halt until the
flood subsided. For the Americans such a delay could
mean facing Cornwallis, who would almost certainly
defeat them and rampage on into Virginia.

When Huger, who was to join Greene and Morgan at
Salisbury, did not arrive, Greene sent him orders to
change his course and make the junction at Guilford
Courthouse, farther north, near the Virginia border. The
general then rode on from Salisbury and rejoined Morgan.

Greene's wisdom in having boats to carry his army
across the large rivers now became apparent. The Yadkin
was a raging torrent at a ford east of Salisbury from the

rains that had fallen during most of the retreat. The cavalry swam their horses over and the infantry crossed in the boats.

Cornwallis had hoped to catch the Americans before they could cross the Yadkin. He burned more of his baggage and sent all his cavalry racing toward the river, but they reached it just as the last of Morgan's force landed on the other side. Cornwallis was unable to pursue them as no more boats were available.

Cornwallis' only recourse was to take his army ten miles up the Yadkin, where Shallow Ford was passable, which would be a serious delay. However, he received a report that the Dan was impassable and not enough boats were at the ferry to carry the Americans across the wide, deep river quickly, so he took the roundabout route, crossed the Yadkin and continued the chase.

From the Yadkin the Americans marched to Guilford Courthouse, where they met Huger's division. His soldiers' clothes were in tatters and many men without shoes were suffering from frostbite. The men were gaunt from scanty rations, as well as their horses, whose harnesses had been patched and mended so many times that they were ready to fall apart. The wagons, jammed with sick men, were so rickety that their wheels wobbled crazily.

Yet these brave men were ready to do battle if Greene ordered it. He wanted to make a stand at Guilford Courthouse, but his officers dissuaded him, feeling that Huger's men must have time to recuperate from their ordeal before fighting. They argued that once they were across the Dan there would be supplies and reinforcements to enable them to turn on Cornwallis and fight him on even terms, if not better, and Greene at last agreed with the officers.

His chief concern now was whether Colonel Carrington had rounded up the boats at the agreed crossing. Cornwallis, of course, was under the impression that there were not enough to enable the Americans to escape.

At Guilford Courthouse, Daniel Morgan who was lame, sick and exhausted, told Greene he must go home. There was many a sad heart among officers and men alike when Morgan painfully hoisted himself onto his horse and set out for his home in Virginia.

The British, having crossed the Yadkin higher up, where its course in that region was southeasterly, were now somewhat to the west of the Americans. Greene sent Otho Williams with the pick of the army—280 of Colonel Washington's cavalry, 280 Continentals and 60 Virginia sharpshooters, with Light Horse Harry Lee's Legion as the rear guard—to put themselves ahead of Cornwallis and harass him.

Greene made no mistake in sending Otho Williams on this mission, for although Tarleton had built his Green Dragoons up to full strength again, Williams and his men were more than a match for him. Using a system of dodging, backtracking and circling the British so that they never knew quite where their enemy was, the Americans would swiftly appear, mow down some of the enemy and vanish. The British were in the position of swatting vainly at a cloud of stinging gadflies they never could hit.

One favorite trick of Williams' was to place men along the road in concealment just ahead of Cornwallis' advance guard, the Green Dragoons and some Hessian jägers.

From their protected hiding places they would pick off some of Tarleton's horses and disappear, thus keeping Cornwallis busy rearranging his column and losing precious time.

Cornwallis, however, was setting an exhausting pace, starting early in the morning and not camping till several hours after dark. The strain was beginning to tell on Williams and his men. At last Greene ordered him to rejoin the main army.

Cornwallis was convinced Greene was heading for the upper, shallower fords of the Dan because of a shortage of boats at the lower, deeper crossing, and the British therefore headed upstream. But when Cornwallis' scouts reported Williams' detachment had ridden off to the east, he realized Greene was going downstream to Boyd's Ferry, after all, and the British commander veered in that direction too.

Cornwallis' army, marching twenty-five miles a day, was gaining on the Americans. They were so close that at one time Light Horse Harry Lee's horsemen of the American rear guard were in sight of the British advance guard. When one night stood between the Americans and Boyd's Ferry, Lee's rear guard reported the British had camped. Greene's almost exhausted army therefore made camp also, but at midnight Cornwallis resumed the chase and the Americans staggered on.

That next morning, approaching Boyd's Ferry, a thick mist obscured the view down the road, making it difficult for Nathanael Greene to see if Carrington had succeeded in rounding up the boats needed for his troops to cross the Dan River.

Fortunately, Colonel Carrington had done a perfect job, not only rounding up plenty of boats for the American troops, but also making sure the British would find none when they got there.

The Americans crossed in safety and slept peacefully in Virginia that night. For Greene it was the greatest triumph of his military career, perhaps the most important feat accomplished during the entire Revolution, for this had been a retreat to victory.

Cornwallis had been badly outgeneraled. Foolishly, he had marched long, weary miles into the gradually closing trap Greene had set for him. He had rid himself of all but the barest essentials of his supplies and equipment, with his main base of supplies, Charleston, South Carolina, about three hundred miles away. The only nearer one, Wilmington, North Carolina, was over two hundred miles distant.

Cornwallis had only one way to redeem his rash blunder. If he could engage Greene in battle and defeat him decisively, Cornwallis could then go on triumphantly into Virginia. But Greene would be ready for that meeting, as soon as his army was rested and strengthened enough to recross the Dan and give battle to the British.

18

Cornwallis' Last Long Road

NATHANAEL GREENE WAITED RESTLESSLY FOR REINFORCE-
ments and supplies. Meanwhile the Dan was falling
rapidly from its flood stage, and might result in an attempt by Cornwallis to cross the river and attack. Greene,
however, was intensely anxious to recross the river and
meet the British in battle on a field of his own choosing.

Cornwallis retired southward and camped at Hillsboro
while he decided what to do. On February 20 Greene
sent Otho Williams and his detachment back over the
river to watch the British. Soon afterward Greene was
reinforced by 600 Virginia riflemen. Although he felt he
needed more men, he decided to go back into North Carolina and harass the enemy until the additional troops he
expected arrived.

Cornwallis' provisions, especially meat, were so low
that his foraging parties had to seize cattle and go from
house to house, taking what food they could find there.
The people, even the Tories, became so resentful that on

February 27 Cornwallis moved southeast, hoping to find
friendlier country. He camped on Alamance Creek, where
a number of converging roads offered escape if Greene
forced him to retreat.

That same day Otho Williams' force, joined by Andrew
Pickens' corps, Lee's Legion and a new corps of mountain
sharpshooters camped not far from Cornwallis. The following day Greene, Huger and the rest of the army
arrived. Greene had about 1,200 men against Cornwallis'

How the opposing British and Americans formed in the decisive
battle of Guilford Courthouse, North Carolina, in 1781.

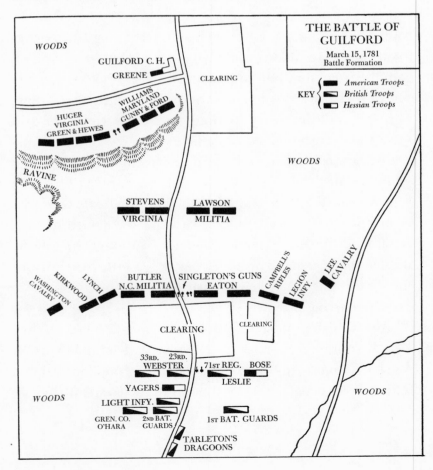

2,000 but the American commander was expecting large reinforcements momentarily.

For ten days the two armies shifted about like a pair of boxers feeling each other out in the ring before closing in for real combat. There were a few skirmishes, but most of both armies rested ten days more. Meanwhile, Steuben sent 400 Continentals and 1,060 North Carolina and 1,639 Virginia militia. Now Greene was ready for battle, and Cornwallis seemed anxious also. But it was Nathanael Greene who chose Guilford Courthouse as the battlefield, the site he had chosen before reaching Virginia.

Greene now had about 4,400 men and four 6-pounder cannon. Although Cornwallis' strength was far less, only the 630 magnificent Maryland and Delaware troops had been in battle before. The outcome at Guilford Courthouse might once more depend upon the reliability of the militia.

The British were camped a dozen miles south of Guilford Courthouse. They started for the battlefield during the night of March 14. Light Horse Harry Lee, whose Legion had been detached to watch Cornwallis, was wakened with the word that the enemy was moving, and he sent a dispatch to warn Greene.

The British did not arrive until about noon the next day, March 15, 1781; meanwhile, Greene formed his army for battle. He had made the best possible choice of his battlefield. Except for the courthouse, on a ridge, and a scattering of farmhouses, it was wilderness. It was quite thickly wooded, save for a clearing by the courthouse and another down the slope where the British were approaching. Beyond the lower clearing was a valley in which a creek flowed.

The fight ranges at close quarters during the battle of Guilford Courthouse.

British cavalry charge Gen. Nathanael Greene's American army at Guilford Courthouse.

Nathanael Greene had been in correspondence with Daniel Morgan in Virginia about the battle. Morgan advised using the same strategy that had been so effective at Cowpens, since Greene too had so many militia.

"Put the militia in the center," Morgan wrote, "with some picked troops in the rear to shoot down the first man that runs. If they fight, you will beat Cornwallis. If not, he will beat you and perhaps cut your regulars to pieces."

So Greene put the North Carolina militia along the upper edge of the lower clearing behind a rail fence; thus the enemy would be exposed to gunfire as they crossed the clearing. On both flanks were riflemen to support the militia; on the far right wing, Colonel Washington's cavalry, and on the far left Lee's mounted Legion.

About three hundred yards behind this first line were more militia, posted at intervals in the woods. Then came the third and strongest line composed of the Virginia, Maryland and Delaware Continentals, where Greene remained during the battle. The four 6-pounder field guns were placed ahead of the first line.

In his orders to the front-line militia, Greene followed Morgan's instructions to his militia at Cowpens: to fire two rounds and then fall back. Greene also let them know they would be shot by the Americans behind them if they ran before getting off those two volleys.

On this bright, cold, clear day, the Americans could see from nearly a mile away the scarlet British uniforms and the flash of their bayonets in the sun. The artillery on both sides instantly went into action. The redcoats deployed into line as they advanced. They were more than two-thirds across the clearing when the whole fence at its up-

per end erupted with a roar into smoke, flame and zing-
ing bullets. Great holes were torn in the scarlet line, but
it kept on steadily. Then it halted, fired a volley and
charged. But as it came nearer, the sight of a long line of
musket muzzles pointed straight at them caused them to
halt abruptly.

But a moment later, at an officer's command, the British moved ahead again. The North Carolina militia then
fired its second deadly volley and, having done its duty,
turned and ran, throwing away its guns. Fortunately,
the fleeing militia ran for the American flanks and thus
caused no disruption in the center of the main line
behind them. The British now crossed the deserted fence,
but enfilading fire coming straight along the scarlet-clad
line cut many down.

The British gained an advantage when part of their line
wheeled to the right and cut Lee's horsemen off from the
battle. The rest of the enemy kept on toward the Virginia
militia on the second line. For a time, however, the Virginians stood fast, giving the British volley for volley, until they finally fell back in good order. Colonel Washington's cavalry and light troops, which had fallen back
to the second line when the militia in front ran, tried to
stem the British advance, but were thrown back.

The Americans were in trouble, and the situation became worse when the right wing of the second line of
militia collapsed and ran, leaving a hole through which
the British and Hessians plunged in a charge on the third,
strongest American line. But the Continentals on the third
line gave the British a volley that caused terrible havoc
and opened gaping holes in the enemy line. They were
then able to drive the redcoats back with bayonets.

The enemy left side was now in such confusion that Greene saw he might rout the whole British army if he threw all his men into a charge. Yet it was a serious risk; if the charge failed, the Americans might be defeated, the terrible weeks of Greene's flight from Cornwallis would go for naught, and the war in the south would be lost, and so Greene decided not to take the chance.

The left side of the second American line, which had held fast, was crumbling now. The British slowly forced the second line back into the woods in the rear of the courthouse, and then wheeled and struck at a Maryland Continental regiment which had been held in reserve in the American rear. The British attack was so intense that even these stout American fighters fled.

The situation seemed grim for the Americans. But Colonel Washington, at the far opposite end of the line, saw what had happened and made a wide sweep with his cavalry to the Continentals' aid, his cavalry fairly cutting their way through the enemy. Another Maryland regiment and the light troops from the first line moved in and drove the now confused attackers back.

The battle had suddenly swung in favor of the Americans. The Continentals' fire was breaking up the center of the British line. Enemy reinforcements came up, but could not stand the ferocity of the Continentals' fire and fell back.

The battle was now a confused melee of hand-to-hand fighting. But from his post in the rear, Cornwallis saw a chance to save his army from defeat. He ordered three British cannon moved to the northwest corner of the field to fire grapeshot into the milling mass of both armies.

An officer pleaded with him not to do it, but Cornwallis

knew it was his only chance to win the battle. Grapeshot
—cast-iron balls enclosed inside a cannonball—could do
frightful execution among the British as well as American
troops. The guns began hurling their deadly balls into the
mass of fighting men, and the Continentals were forced
back. Cornwallis called for one more charge. Nathanael
Greene now had to make another agonizing decision—
should he try to stop this all-important British attack?

The decision was worthy of Greene's skill as a general
—he ordered a retreat. All battles are not lost by the side
that retires, and Greene had accomplished his purpose.
The slaughter among the British troops during the battle
had been terrible, far worse than the American losses.
Cornwallis had won the battle of Guilford Courthouse,
but the victory can only be compared to Howe's rash
assaults on Bunker Hill. Indeed, when the news of Guilford Courthouse reached London, Charles James Fox
remarked, "Another such victory would destroy the British army."

Cornwallis had lost over one-fourth of his 1,900 men.
On the field, 93 were killed and many of the 439 wounded
died later. Of his officers, 29 British and Hessians were
killed or wounded. There were 78 Americans killed and
183 wounded, and the militia had fled, not to return, but
Greene still had an overwhelming superiority in numbers.

Although great credit must be given to the British for
their success in attacking so large a force, and to Cornwallis for brilliant generalship during the battle, nevertheless,
Cornwallis' chase after Greene was perhaps the greatest
single mistake made by a British general during the war.
After Guilford Courthouse he was too weak to fight again,

his army almost completely without supplies, and nearly all the baggage sacrificed in this wilderness chase across the Carolinas.

The only possible course of action for Cornwallis was to try to reach his coastal base at Wilmington, North Carolina. The exhausted, hungry, tentless British army set out, pursued for a time by Greene, who finally decided to abandon the chase and strike at the British outposts in South Carolina. On August 7 Cornwallis and his men slogged into Wilmington.

During the campaign Greene waged in South Carolina, he lost every battle of any importance. First, heading to strike at Camden, he was beaten at Hobkirk's Hill April 25, 1781, by a smaller British force. Nevertheless, as he advanced again to attack Camden, he wrote his friend the French ambassador to the United States: "We fight, get beat, rise, fight again."

Colonel Lord Rawdon was in command at Camden, with only 900 men. Although they had beaten 1,400 Americans, most of them Continentals, at Hobkirk's Hill, Rawdon's supplies were scanty and a siege by the Americans might be disastrous. Fearing such an event, Rawdon evacuated the post on May 10 and so Greene won Camden without fighting a battle.

Meanwhile, Light Horse Harry Lee and Francis Marion besieged the British post of Fort Motte. They sent a storm of flaming arrows into it, setting the roofs of its buildings afire, and on May 12 it surrendered. Lee then joined Andrew Pickens, who was besieging Augusta, and it too surrendered soon thereafter on June 6.

Ninety-Six was now the only important British outpost

left in South Carolina, and Greene had already laid siege
to it. After nearly a month of intense fighting in fierce summer heat, Greene was forced to raise the siege and withdraw when Rawdon arrived with British reinforcements.
Rawdon, however, realized Ninety-Six could not be held
for long and he burned and abandoned it.

Rawdon, who was ill, returned to England, leaving
Lieut. Col. Alexander Stewart in command. Greene and
his army fell on Stewart's camp at Eutaw Springs in
southeastern South Carolina on September 8. This was a
battle the Americans should have won and thought they
had after capturing 300 British, leaving only about 500
organized enemy soldiers on the field. Foolishly, the
Americans began pillaging the enemy camp, when the
500 British charged in and forced Greene's army to withdraw. But Stewart had lost over forty percent of his army
and had to retreat to Charleston, the only place of importance left in British hands in South Carolina.

As for North Carolina, only Wilmington remained as a
British supply base. Cornwallis considered moving the
1,400 men there to Charleston, but if he advanced from
Charleston and tried to recover the British outposts he
might find himself in the same trap Greene had set for
him in the chase through the Carolinas. On April 24,
Cornwallis' army started the long march toward Virginia,
hoping to draw Greene after him, but the American commander was too smart for that.

The situation for the Americans in Virginia was not
good. Benedict Arnold, having escaped capture after his
treason at West Point, had obtained a British brigadier
general's commission, and Clinton had sent him to Virginia with about 1,600 troops. For a time Arnold spread

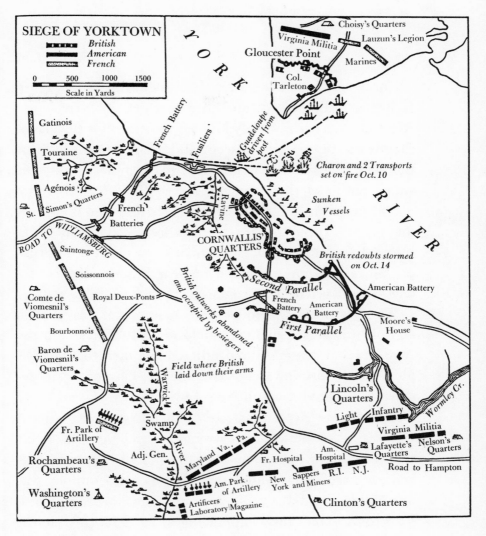

YORK

Choisy's Quarters

Virginia Militia

Lauzun's Legion

Gloucester Point

Marines

Col. Tarleton

Guadeloupe driven from post

Charon and 2 Transports set on fire Oct. 10

Gatinois

Touraine

Agénois

St. Simon's Quarters

French Battery

Fusiliers

French Batteries

Sunken Vessels

RIVER

CORNWALLIS' QUARTERS

Ravine

ROAD TO WILLIAMSBURG

Saintonge

British redoubts stormed on Oct. 14

Soissonnois

Comte de Viomesnil's Quarters

Royal Deux-Ponts

Second Parallel

American Battery

French Battery

American Battery

Moore's House

Bourbonnois

Baron de Viomesnil's Quarters

British outworks abandoned and occupied by besiegers

First Parallel

Field where British laid down their arms

Warwick River

Lincoln's Quarters

Light Infantry

Virginia Militia

Wormley Cr.

Fr. Park of Artillery

Swamp

Adj. Gen.

Maryland Va. Pa.

Fr. Hospital

Am. Hospital

Lafayette's Quarters

Nelson's Quarters

Rochambeau's Quarters

Am. Park of Artillery

New York

Sappers and Miners

R.I. N.J.

Road to Hampton

Washington's Quarters

Artificers Laboratory Magazine

Clinton's Quarters

A map of the British, American and French positions during the siege of Yorktown, Virginia, in which America gained final victory in the Revolution.

terror through the state with his raids that wreaked destruction in the coastal area. Washington sent Lafayette to Virginia with 1,200 troops in the hope of capturing and hanging Arnold. But the wily traitor eluded Lafayette. When Cornwallis arrived in Virginia on May 20 he took over command from Arnold.

Cornwallis' only superior in America at this time was Sir Henry Clinton, the commander in chief, in New York. After the war each bitterly blamed the other for the loss of the Revolution. Clinton seems far more responsible for the decisive events that occurred in Virginia. Cornwallis started off well there, having forced Lafayette to retire northward. But then, just as Lafayette obtained reinforcements and turned back, Cornwallis received an order from Clinton to send 3,000 of his troops to New York by sea, since Washington's army and a French force under Gen. Jean Rochambeau threatened to attack him.

Whether the 3,000 troops were as important to Clinton as to Cornwallis seems extremely doubtful, since Clinton then changed his mind and ordered the men to Philadelphia. But before the troops could leave, Clinton again decided he wanted them in New York; finally he sent word he would not need them at all. Clinton then ordered Cornwallis to establish a strong position at Old Point Comfort and try to occupy Yorktown as well. British engineers advised Cornwallis that Old Point Comfort was unsuitable for defense, so he put his whole army into Yorktown except for a supporting force of 700 just across the York River.

After all this vacillation, Clinton committed a blunder that seems unexplainable, and which sealed Britain's fate in America. Washington had made plans to attack Clinton in New York, but after he and Rochambeau had carefully reconnoitered the British defenses, they found them too strong.

The two allied generals then learned that Adm. François de Grasse, with a powerful French fleet, was

leaving the West Indies for Chesapeake Bay. If he arrived
as planned he could prevent Cornwallis from getting out
of Yorktown by sea. Washington then decided to move
part of his army south along with the French and take
Cornwallis. He sent word to Lafayette to keep the British
troops bottled up in Yorktown from the land side at all
costs.

The success of Washington's plan hung upon one thing:
the Franco-American army must move south without
Clinton's knowledge of the departure; otherwise the British commander would instantly send a powerful force by
sea to reinforce Cornwallis.

This situation was Assunpink Creek all over again,
except that in this case the fate of the American Revolution was at stake. Washington made the most elaborate
preparations to deceive Clinton. He concentrated his
army along the Kill van Kull, the waterway between
Staten Island and New Jersey, as though the attack on
New York City would come from that direction. Large
supply depots were set up in the area and a great flotilla
of boats assembled along the Jersey shore, with the army
encamped nearby.

The part of the force headed for Yorktown—about
2,000 of Washington's army and Rochambeau's French
force of about 4,800—first marched up the Hudson. This
army had remained north of New York, so it crossed westward at Stony Point, then swung south behind the Palisades. Presumably Clinton knew of this maneuver but
thought the attack might come from that direction instead
of Staten Island.

It seems incredible but Clinton does not appear to have

had scouts to inform him that the Franco-American army had turned south, and not until a week later, September 2, did he find out. He immediately sent 7,000 troops to Cornwallis by sea, but by that time it was too late. At this point he could easily have moved against the 3,000 troops of the American army left under command of Maj. Gen. William Heath at the Hudson Highlands, and destroyed them, which would have been a crippling blow even after Yorktown, but Clinton did nothing.

Describing the siege and battle of Yorktown is really not necessary, for Cornwallis' men fought bravely and well, and their defeat reflects no disgrace upon him or any of the British and Hessian soldiers. Their fate was decided when de Grasse's French fleet inflicted so much damage on Adm. Thomas Graves' fleet off the Virginia capes that the British ships had to go to New York for repairs, leaving Cornwallis helpless to escape from Yorktown by sea.

On October 17, 1781, the anniversary of Burgoyne's surrender at Saratoga, Cornwallis ceased hostilities and asked for a meeting to settle terms, although the official surrender took place on October 19. Tradition has it that the British and Hessian bands played an English song called "The World Turned Upside Down." There was sporadic fighting after Yorktown and hostilities did not officially cease until April 19, 1783, but with Yorktown's capitulation the war was over.

Who was most to blame for Britain's loss of a war that should have been a quick and easy victory? In part, the generals—Gage, Howe, Burgoyne, Cornwallis, and Clinton—were to blame. Each made his mistakes, some

Gen. Lord Cornwallis surrenders his British army at Yorktown,
ending the American Revolution.

graver than others, and together they combined to bring defeat. But what of the powers behind them in London? What of King George III, Lord George Germain and other important figures who carried on the war from the British capital?

Events that happened in the royal palace, in Parliament, in the offices of the officials connected with the war in America also effected the outcome of the war. More than one of the leaders in England must share grave responsibility for the British defeat.

19

The British Government Culprits

MANY BRITISH GOVERNMENT OFFICIALS MUST SHARE THE blame for losing a war they had every means of winning. But if the greatest blame is to rest upon one man it must be His Majesty King George III.

One historian calls George III a simple soul. He liked simple pleasures, and his love for gardening caused his subjects to call him "Farmer George." When he was born June 4, 1738, his grandfather, George II, was on the throne. Both George I and George II were born in Germany and were Electors (kings) of the German state of Hanover, which explains why George III hired so many German mercenaries to fight in America.

George III's mother, Princess Augusta of the German state of Saxe-Coburg, was largely responsible for making him the kind of man and king he was. As a boy he was kept completely isolated from the world, yet she constantly told him: "George, when you come to the throne, be King!" His father, the heir to the throne, died in 1751 while George II still ruled, so it was the grandson who became King on George II's death in 1760. And while George III ruled it was not safe for anyone to cross him.

As a boy, George was poorly educated and very backward. He spoke both English and German, knew a little Italian, but his general knowledge, especially of history was sketchy, and his grammar and spelling were atrocious.

But another, more serious handicap appeared as early as 1765 when he suffered a brief attack of insanity. After the Revolution, these attacks became more frequent and severe, and for nine years, from 1811 to his death in 1820, he was hopelessly insane. His son, who became George IV, ruled for him as regent.

Yet George III did manage to overcome much of his ignorance of worldly matters. He acquired a keen judgment of the character of his ministers and others close to him, and of how to use all the power the Crown gave him.

The Whigs, the political party that favored moderation toward the American colonies, were in power in Parliament as the American Revolution approached. In fact, while the loyalists in America were called by the name of the British opposition party, the Tories, the American rebels were often known as Whigs.

George III, who favored harsh measures against the rebellious colonies, was determined to weaken the English Whigs' power. He did it by transferring patronage out of the hands of his cabinet ministers—some were Whigs, some Tories—and using it himself. Patronage, the power to hand out jobs in the government, was then, as today, a powerful political privilege. By the use of patronage, George III built up a kind of strong, separate party in Parliament, known as "the King's friends," and to be a King's friend was very desirable.

In the years preceding the Revolution, George III strongly supported the oppressive laws that brought on the war with the colonies. Plenty of statesmen wanted Britain to appease the Americans, but the King, using his "friends," prevented it. Although he had graceful manners he was nevertheless a cold, petulant ruler who considered it a personal insult when anyone opposed him.

George III was sure British might would subdue the colonies quickly, as indeed it should have. When the war dragged on, he became extremely bitter against the Americans and more determined than ever to crush them. It was one of George III's policies to make use of Indians in the war, a policy that led Burgoyne to make one of the tragic mistakes of his invasion of 1777. Burgoyne's surrender at Saratoga came as a stunning blow to George III, but it only increased his determination to beat the Americans. Unfortunately, most of the members of his cabinet were not especially competent in the parts they played in the waging of the war, one important reason Britain lost the Revolution.

Undoubtedly the worst of them was Lord George Germain, Secretary of State for the Colonies in the newly organized Colonial Department. His job and that of his subordinates was to run the war in America and win it. Germain was highly intelligent, energetic and able to sweep aside at least some of the red tape in which government departments are so often entangled. There was much inefficiency in his own department, however, partly due to nepotism—when high officials place their relatives in jobs for which they are usually not qualified.

Other government departments interfered with Germain's plans or did not cooperate with the Colonial Department properly. For example, store ships sailing for America were supposed to be protected by convoys of warships. Too often, when these ships were ready to sail, the British Admiralty failed to furnish an armed convoy, and often enough American privateers captured these British vessels with the much needed supplies for the troops.

Germain's reputation before being appointed Secretary of State undoubtedly worked against him. During the Seven Years War (called the French and Indian War in America), he disobeyed the orders of the commander of

The greatest blame for Britain's loss of the American Revolution rests upon stubborn King George III, shown here as the youthful king a few years after he came to the throne in 1760.
NEW YORK PUBLIC LIBRARY PICTURE COLLECTION

Long residence in America and incompetence made British Gen. Thomas Gage, first of the British commanders in chief during the Revoluton, unfitted to win a quick victory before American efforts could gain strength and momentum.

an Anglo-German army at the important battle of Minden in Germany, preventing a decisive victory over the French. Many British government officials wanted him tried for cowardice, but Germain had enough influence to prevent it.

Although Germain always claimed he was innocent and had failed to obey because the orders at Minden were not precise enough, George II informed him he had no further use for his military services. Unlike his grandfather, George III thought highly enough of Germain, who had not been dismissed from the army, to appoint him to run the war against America. Many British officials questioned the wisdom of naming him Secretary of State for the Colonies. The most serious criticism of Germain is that the Colonial Secretary failed to select the best generals available to go to America, and sent officers that were all fairly junior to others with longer and more distinguished war service.

Certainly there is reason to doubt Burgoyne's ability to lead the 1777 invasion from Canada. Gentleman

Johnny knew how to train troops and gain their respect and affection, but too much of his time in the army
before the Revolution was spent at posts where he had
little to do and could spend much time in London leading
the life of a dissolute English gentleman. His only real
distinction in battle had been his brilliant capture of
Valencia d'Alcantara in Spain in 1762. However, Germain
was not responsible for Burgoyne's appointment to command the 1777 invasion. Since Burgoyne had been along
on the 1776 attempt on Ticonderoga, Germain was almost
as bitter against him as he was against the commander of
the expedition, Sir Guy Carleton. But Burgoyne's good
friend, George III, saw that he was named to the command in 1777.

General Gage, of course, was a poor choice. Although
he had had much fighting experience in America during
the French and Indian War, he had been too long in
America, had an American wife, and was almost American
himself. Such a man, liking Americans, could hardly have
had as much enthusiasm for punishing them as a general
less well acquainted with them. He certainly was a miserable failure in Boston, since responsibility as commander in chief for the Bunker Hill "victory" fell squarely
on his shoulders.

In the case of Sir William Howe, being junior to other
British generals was an advantage, for although he was
less than fifty years old when he was sent to America, he
had a brilliant military record. In America, during the
French and Indian War, he had distinguished himself at
the successful siege of the mighty French fortress of
Louisbourg in what is now part of Nova Scotia, under the

famous Maj. Gen. Jeffrey Amherst. At that time, Brig. Gen. James Wolfe, who was with the expedition, called the then Major Howe's men "the best trained battalion in all America."

Later, in 1759, when the British army commanded by Wolfe, now major general, attacked Quebec, it was Howe who had the most dangerous task of all, leading the first troops up the steep, rocky cliffs to the Plains of Abraham, outside Quebec, where Wolfe died in beating the French and won all of Canada for Britain. Howe continued to fight in this bloody war; one historian said that in it "no officer had a more brilliant record of service than Howe." Howe's record in the Revolution included some glaring and inexplicable failures at times when he might have won final victory for Britain, but Germain can scarcely be blamed for naming a general with such an outstanding record to command in America.

Sir Henry Clinton certainly was a junior general when he came to Boston in 1775, for he was only about thirty-seven years old, and his military record was far from shining. He had been wounded in the Seven Years War, having gained no special glory; therefore his promotion to major general at about twenty-eight seems to have been due to his important political connections. Clinton's appointment was a mistake by the British government considering Clinton's record in America, which was little short of disgraceful, with the exception of his capture of Charleston.

Nor was Cornwallis' record before he came to America outstanding. He had seen a good deal of active service in Europe, but from 1762 to 1775 he held several posts that could hardly be called military ones. In America, his failure to catch Washington in the chase across New Jersey was Howe's fault, not his. Yet his failure to strike quickly at Assunpink Creek, and his grievous mistake in chasing Greene through the Carolinas were his own responsibility. There were generals in the British army in England better suited than he to high command in America.

One British general in America stands out, though he is not widely known. Sir Guy Carleton had a long and outstanding military record during the French and Indian War under Amherst and Wolfe, and was also a highly competent statesman and twice governor of the Province of Quebec.

Carleton's expedition up Lake Champlain in the fall of 1776 to capture Fort Ticonderoga has already been described. When he was delayed in reaching the fort until late in the season he decided not to risk a long siege in midwinter, far from his base of supplies. Germain was enraged at what he considered Carleton's failure, though the general's decision may well have been right. Carleton had none of Gentleman Johnny Burgoyne's rash daring, but was similar to Nathanael Greene, who would not take a risk he considered too great.

In the winter of 1775–76, Benedict Arnold led troops from Cambridge through the Maine and Quebec wilderness on his frightful and famous march to meet Brig. Gen. Richard Montgomery, coming down the St. Lawrence, outside Quebec. Carleton saved the city by quick and decisive action during an American night attack in a raging blizzard. This was a stroke of genius, since the Americans, led by Daniel Morgan after Montgomery had been killed and Arnold put out of action, came within a hair's breadth of taking the mighty fortress on its rock high above the river. And with Quebec captured, in all probability the rest of Canada would have fallen also.

If Germain had put aside his resentment against Carleton and appointed him to command the British army in America, the story of the Revolution might have been different. The performance of the other generals, however, left much to be desired, and this must be charged against the King, Germain and others who may have had a hand in naming the British generals to crush America. The combination of factors that contributed largely to the British loss were therefore the appointment of generals who blundered or failed to act swiftly and sometimes not at all, a Colonial Department ridden with incompetence, interference and lack of cooperation by other departments, and a stubborn and rather ignorant King. As with most wars, the element of human error and ego was much more a determining factor than military expertise or sheer number of troops.

Bibliography

Adams, Charles Francis. "The Battle of Long Island." *American Historical Review* 1 (1895).

Adams, John and Abigail. *Familiar Letters of John Adams and His Wife Abigail Adams during the Revolution.* New York: Hurd & Houghton, 1876.

Alden, John Richard. *General Gage in America.* Baton Rouge: Louisiana State University Press, 1948.

Allen, Ethan. *A Narrative of Colonel Ethan Allen's Captivity.* Burlington, Vt.: Chauncey Goodrich, 1846.

Anderson, Troyer Steele. *The Command of the Howe Brothers during the American Revolution.* New York: Oxford University Press, 1936.

Batchelder, Samuel F. "Burgoyne and His Officers in Cambridge." *Cambridge Historical Society Proceedings* 10 (1926).

Belcher, Henry. "Burgoyne." *New York State Historical Association Proceedings* 12 (1913).

Bill, Alfred Hoyt. *Valley Forge: the Making of an Army.* New York: Harper, 1952.

Billias, George Athan. *George Washington's Generals.* New York: Morrow, 1964.

Blythe, Le Gette, and Brockman, Charles Raven. *Hornets' Nest: the Story of Charlotte and Mecklenburg County*. Charlotte, N.C.: McNally & Loftin, 1961.

Boatner, Mark M. III. *Encyclopedia of the American Revolution*. New York: McKay, 1969.

Bolton, Reginald Pelham. *The Defense and Reduction of Mt. Washington*. New York: Empire State Society, Sons of the American Revolution, 1902.

Botkin, B. A. (ed.). *A Treasury of New England Folklore*. New York: Crown, 1947.

Boyd, Thomas. *Light-horse Harry Lee*. New York: Scribner, 1931.

Breck, Samuel. *Historical Sketch of the Continental Paper Money*. Philadelphia: John C. Clark, 1843.

Bridenbaugh, Carl and Jessie. *Rebels and Gentlemen: Philadelphia in the Age of Franklin*. New York: Oxford University Press, 1962.

Chidsey, Donald Barr. *Valley Forge*. New York: Crown, 1959.

Chittenden, Lucius F. *The Capture of Ticonderoga*. Rutland, Vt.: Tuttle, 1872.

Clinton, Sir Henry. *Observations on Lord Cornwallis' Answer*. Philadelphia: John Campbell, 1866.

Crockett, Walter Hill. *Vermont, the Green Mountain State*. New York: Century History Co., 1921.

Davis, Burke. *The Cowpens-Guilford Courthouse Campaign*. Philadelphia: Lippincott, 1962.

Dearborn, Nathaniel. *Boston Notions*. Boston: Printed by the author, 1848.

De Fonblanque, Edward Barrington. *Political and Military Episodes in the Latter Half of the Eighteenth Century Derived from the Life of the Honorable John Burgoyne*. London: Macmillan, 1876.

De Lancey, Edward F. "The Capture of Mt. Washington." Paper read before the New York Historical Society, 1876.

Downey, Fairfax. *Sound of the Guns*. New York: McKay, 1955.

Drake, Francis S. *Life and Correspondence of Henry Knox*. Boston: Samuel G. Drake, 1873.

————. *The Town of Roxbury*. Roxbury, Mass.: Published by the author, 1878.

Drake, Samuel Adams. *Old Boston Taverns and Tavern Clubs*. Boston: W. A. Butterfield, 1917.

————. *Old Landmarks and Historic Personages of Boston*. Boston: Little, Brown, 1900.

Drake, Samuel G. *History and Antiquities of Boston*. Boston: Luther Slivens, 1856.

Dupuy, R. Ernest and Trevor N. *The Compact History of the Revolutionary War*. New York: Hawthorn, 1963.

Earle, Alice Morse. *Home Life in Colonial Days*. New York: Grosset & Dunlap, 1898.

Ehrlich, Blake. *London on the Thames*. Boston: Little, Brown, 1966.

Ellis, George E. "General Burgoyne in Boston." *Massachusetts Historical Society Proceedings* 14 (March, 1876).

Faris, John T. *The Romance of Old Philadelphia*. Philadelphia: Lippincott, 1918.

Field, Thomas W. "The Battle of Long Island." *Memoirs of the Long Island Historical Society* 2 (1894).

Forbes, Esther. *Paul Revere and the World He Lived In*. Boston: Houghton Mifflin, 1942.

French, Allen. *The Taking of Ticonderoga in 1775; the British Story*. Cambridge: Harvard University Press, 1928.

Frothingham, Richard. *History of the Seige of Boston*. Boston: Little, Brown, 1873.

Fry, Plantagenet Somerset. *Rulers of Britain*. London: Paul Hamlyn, 1967.

Graydon, Alexander. *Memoirs of His Own Time*. Philadelphia: Lindsay & Blackiston, 1846.

Greene, Francis Vinton. *General Greene*. New York: D. Appleton, 1879.

Greene, George Washington. *Life of Nathanael Greene*. New York: Hurd & Houghton, 1871.

Guedalla, Philip. *Fathers of the Revolution*. Chatauqua, N.Y.: Chatauqua Press, 1926.

Hall, Edward Hagamann. *Fort Washington and Its Related Fortifications.* New York: Empire State Society, Sons of the American Revolution, 1902.

Harazti, Zoltan. "Besieging Boston With a Dwindling Army." *Bulletin, Boston Public Library* 7 (May, 1932).

————. "The Last Stages of the Siege of Boston." *Bulletin, Boston Public Library* 7 (September, 1932).

Hemenway, Abby Maria. *Vermont Historical Gazetteer.* Ludlow, Vt.: Published by the author, 1861.

Higginbotham, Don. *The War of American Independence.* New York: Macmillan, 1971.

Holden, Clarence E. *Local History Sketches.* Whitehall, N.Y.: Whitehall Times, March, 1916–July, 1918.

Hudleston, F. J. *Gentleman Johnny Burgoyne.* Garden City, N.Y.: Garden City Publishing Co., 1927.

Johnson, Gerald W. *Pattern for Liberty: the Story of Old Philadelphia.* New York: McGraw-Hill, 1952.

Johnson, William. *Sketches of the Life and Correspondence of Nathanael Greene.* Charleston, S.C.: Printed for the author, 1832.

Joyce, J. St. George (ed.). *Story of Philadelphia.* © Harry B. Joseph, 1919.

Kent, Louise Andrews, and Tarshis, Elizabeth Kent. *In Good Old Colony Times.* Boston: Houghton Mifflin, 1941.

Ketchum, Richard M. *The Battle for Bunker Hill.* London: Cresset Press, 1963.

Lefferts, Charles M. *Uniforms of the American, Canadian, British, French and German Armies in the War of the American Revolution.* New York: New York Historical Society, 1926.

Lossing, Benson J. *The American Revolution and the War of 1812.* New York: New York Book Concern, 1875.

Mackesy, Piers. "British Strategy in the War of American Independence." *Yale Review* 52 (Summer, 1936).

Malone, Dumas (ed.). *Dictionary of American Biography.* New York: Scribner, 1933.

Mann, Albert W. *Walks and Talks about Historic Boston.* Boston: Mann Publishing Co., 1916.

Miller, John C. *Origins of the American Revolution.* Boston: Little, Brown, 1943.

Morgan, George. *History of Philadelphia.* Philadelphia: Historical Publication Society in Philadelphia, 1926.

Mumby, Frank Arthur. *George III and the American Revolution.* London: Constable & Co., Ltd., 1924.

Partridge, Bellamy. *Sir Billy Howe.* London: Longmans, Green, 1932.

Phillips, Hugh. *Mid-Georgian London.* Boston: Collins, 1964.

Pottinger, David T. "John Burgoyne, Politician, Dandy, Man of Letters." *Cambridge Historical Society Proceedings* 22 (1932, 1933).

Riedesel, Frederika. *Letters and Journals Relating to the War of the American Revolution.* Albany: Joel Munsell, 1887.

Savage, Edward H. *Police Records and Recollections or Boston by Daylight and Gaslight for 240 Years.* Boston: John P. Dale & Co., 1873.

Scharf, Thomas, and Westcott, Thompson. *History of Philadelphia.* Philadelphia: L. N. Everts & Co., 1884.

Simms, W. Gilmore (ed.). *The Life of Nathanael Greene.* New York: George F. Coolidge & Bros., 1849.

Smith, Justin H. *Our Struggle for the 14th Colony.* New York: Putnam, 1907.

Spargo, John. *Ethan Allen at Ticonderoga.* Rutland, Vt.: Tuttle Co., 1926.

————. *The Stars and Stripes in 1777.* Bennington, Vt.: Bennington Battle Monument and Historical Association, 1928.

Spector, Margaret Marion. *The American Department of the British Government, 1768–1782.* New York: Columbia University Press, 1940.

Stephen, Leslie and Lee, S. (eds.). *The Dictionary of National Biography*. Oxford: Oxford University Press, 1960.

Stoddard, G. R. *Ticonderoga, Past and Present*. Albany: Weed, Parsons, 1873.

Stone, Frederick D. "The Struggle for the Delaware." *Narrative and Critical History of America*, vol. 6. Boston: Houghton Mifflin, 1898.

Stone, William L. *The Campaign of Lieut. Gen. John Burgoyne and the Expedition of Lieut. Col. Barry St. Leger*. Albany: Joel Munsell, 1877.

Stoudt, John Joseph. *Ordeal at Valley Forge*. Philadelphia: University of Pennsylvania Press, 1963.

Swett, S. *History of Bunker Hill Battle*. Boston: Monroe & Francis, 1827.

Tarleton, Banastre. *A History of the Campaigns of 1780 and 1781 in the Southern Provinces of North America*. New York: *The New York Times* and Arno Press, 1968.

Thayer, Theodore. *Nathanael Greene, Strategist of the Revolution*. New York: Twayne Publishers, 1960.

Thwing, Annie Haven. *The Crooked and Narrow Streets of the Town of Boston*. Boston: Marshall Jones Co., 1920.

Tompkins, Daniel Augustus. *History of Mecklenburg County and the City of Charlotte*. Charlotte, N.C.: Observer Printing House, 1903.

Treacy, M. F. *Prelude to Yorktown: the Southern Campaign of Nathanael Greene*. Chapel Hill: University of North Carolina Press, 1963.

Trevelyan, George Otto. *The American Revolution*. New York: Longmans, Green, 1899.

Tudor, William. *Deacon Tudor's Diary*. Boston: William Spooner, 1896.

Van de Water, Frederic F. *Reluctant Republic*. New York: John Day, 1941.

Walpole, Horace. *The Letters of Horace Walpole*. Oxford: Clarendon Press, 1904.

Ward, Christopher. *The War of the Revolution*. New York: Macmillan, 1952.

Wheildon, William W. *Siege and Evacuation of Boston and Charlestown*. Boston: Lee & Shepard, 1876.

Willcox, William B. (ed.). *The American Rebellion: Sir Henry Clinton's Narrative of the Campaigns, 1775–1782*. New Haven: Yale University Press, 1954.

————. "Why Did the British Lose the American Revolution?" *Michigan Alumnus Quarterly Review*, vol. 62, no. 21 (August, 1956).

Winsor, Justin (ed.). *The Memorial History of Boston*. Boston: Ticknor & Co., 1881.

Wyatt, Frederick, and Willcox, William B. "Sir Henry Clinton, a Psychological Exploration in History." *William & Mary Quarterly*, ser. 3, vol. 16, no. 15 (January, 1959).

Suggested Further Reading

Since this book covers almost all the American Revolution, it is difficult to recommend books for further reading by those who are interested in more details on various phases of or the entire war, and such a list would be a long one.

First, however, for those who would like to study the entire Revolution in more detail, one of the most complete, accurate and carefully researched books is *Encyclopedia of the American Revolution*, by Mark M. Boatner, III, himself an army officer and graduate of the U.S. Military Academy. Another excellent book in this category is the two-volume *The War of the Revolution*, by Christopher Ward. For a somewhat briefer but complete account of the entire war, *The Compact History of the Revolutionary War*, by two other West Pointers, R. Ernest and Trevor N. Dupuy, is also highly recommended.

Biographies of the British generals are not likely to be found in most cases except in large reference libraries.

However, *Gentleman Johnny Burgoyne*, by F. J. Hudleston, is written in humorous style, is easy, amusing reading and quite accurate. *Sir Billy Howe*, by Bellamy Partridge, may be found in some libraries and is an excellent study of Sir William Howe. *General Gage in America*, by John Richard Alden, may also be in many libraries and is excellent. Full-length biographies of Sir Henry Clinton will be hard to find and there is no good full-length one of Earl Charles Cornwallis.

Index

A

Acteon, HMS, 35
Adams, John, 123
Allen, Ethan, 9–15, 88, 159
André, Capt. John, 123, 124
Armand, Col. Charles, 151, 152
Armstrong, Brig. Gen. John, 114
Army, French, 196, 197
Arnold, Maj. Gen. Benedict, 5, 14, 40, 68, 74, 78, 102, 103, 105, 106, 110, 124, 157, 194, 195, 208, 209
Augusta, Princess, 201, 202

B

Battles
  Assunpink Creek, 60, 61, 63, 79, 197
  Bemis Heights, 100, 101, 105–107
  Bennington, 80, 89, 91–98, 100, 110
  Brandywine, 112, 113, 116

  Breed's Hill. *See* Bunker Hill
  Bunker Hill, 3, 22, 23, 39, 45, 48, 52, 90, 163
  Camden, 150–56, 158–60, 171
  Charleston, 30–36, 38, 127, 138–44, 147, 156
  Concord, 2, 4, 16, 21
  Cowpens, 171, 173–76, 178, 189
  Eutaw Springs, 194
  Freeman's Farm, 101–104
  Germantown, 113–16
  Guilford Courthouse, 187–92
  Harlem Heights, 48–50
  Hobkirk's Hill, 193
  Hubbardton, 79, 80, 87, 90
  King's Mountain, 163, 173
  Lexington, 6, 16, 21
  Long Island, 37–46
  Monmouth Courthouse, 129
  Oriskany, 72, 73
  Princeton, 59–64, 90
  Saratoga, 99–110, 198, 203
  Savannah, 131, 132

Trenton, 39, 56–58, 90
Waxhaws, 144, 145, 160
White Plains, 50, 51
Yorktown, 196–98
Baum, Lt. Col., Friedrich, 88–95
Beattie's Ford, 179
Boston, siege of, 2, 3, 5, 17–27, 108, 109
Boyd's Ferry, 183
Brant, Joseph, 69, 70, 74
Breymann, Lt. Col. Heinrich, 95–97, 106
Bristol, HMS, 34
British government, 203, 204, 209
Broad River, 171
Brunswickers, 3, 39, 67, 68, 88, 94–97, 102, 106
Buford, Col. Abraham, 144
Burgoyne, Maj. Gen. John, 6, 7, 22, 39, 64–67, 69, 74–81, 83–85, 87, 88, 91, 97, 99–110, 112, 198, 203, 205, 206
Burke, Edmund, 77

Camden, S.C., 144, 147, 149, 160, 193
Campbell, Lt. Col. Archibald, 131, 132
Campbell, Col. William, 163
Canada invasion, 90
Canadian troops, 67, 68, 102
Carleton, Gen. Sir Guy, 14, 64–67, 206, 208, 209
Carrington, Col. Edward, 168, 182–184
Castleton, 10, 80
Caswell, Maj. Gen. Richard, 150
Catawba River, 169, 170, 178, 179

Champlain, Lake, 8, 81
Charleston, S.C., 184, 194
Charlotte, N.C., 165, 166, 168, 169
Cheraw Hill, 168, 169
Chew house, 115, 123
Clinton, Gen. Sir Henry, 6, 28–32, 38, 39, 42, 44, 55, 103, 104, 124, 127–31, 135–39, 141, 143–45, 194–98, 207
Congress, Continental, 1, 5, 55, 86, 90, 113, 123, 127, 133, 148, 165
Connecticut troops, 46
Continental Army, 3, 37, 70, 99, 111, 125, 133, 134, 140, 147, 150, 152, 167, 169, 173–75, 182, 187, 189, 190–93
Conway Cabal, 120, 121, 148
Conway, Maj. Gen. Thomas, 120
Corne, St. Luc de la, 85
Cornwallis, Gen. Earl Charles, 42, 43, 53–56, 58, 59, 61–63, 113, 139, 144–46, 151–53, 155, 157, 160, 164, 167–70, 177–88, 190–98, 207, 208
Cowan's Ford, 179

Dan River, 168, 180, 183–85
Dartmouth, Lord William, 14
Davidson, Col. William, 179, 180
Deep River, N.C., 148
Deep Run, N.C., 147, 148
Delaplace, Capt. William, 9, 13, 14
Delaware River, 56, 58–60
Delaware troops, 45, 146, 150, 152, 155, 173, 175, 187, 189
d'Estaing, Adm. Count Charles, 129, 130, 134, 135

Dorchester Heights, 24, 26, 27, 79

E

Erskine, Brig. Gen. Sir William, 61

F

Feltman, Lt. Jocelyn, 9
Ferguson, Maj. Patrick, 161–64
Flag, American, first in battle, 93
Forts
 Ann, 83
 Clinton, 104
 Edward, 82, 83, 87, 99, 145
 Johnson, 31, 139
 Lee, 51, 53, 54
 Miller, 100, 101
 Montgomery, 103, 104
 Motte, 193
 Moultrie. *See* Fort Sullivan
 Stanwix, 69–71, 73, 74
 Sullivan, 31–34, 36, 140
 Ticonderoga, 8–15, 26, 27, 64, 77–79, 81
 Washington, 50–53
Fox, Charles James, 192
Fraser, Brig. Gen. Simon, 79, 80, 102
Fraser, Capt. Simon, 92
French alliance, 5, 128

G

Gadsden, Lt. Gov. Christopher, 142, 143
Gage, Lt. Gen. Thomas, 4, 6, 14, 22–24, 199, 206
Gansevoort, Col. Peter, 70, 71, 73
Gates, Maj. Gen. Horatio, 78,
80, 85, 86, 99–106, 108, 110, 120, 121, 148–53, 156–59, 165, 166
George I, 201
George II, 201, 202, 205
George III, 3, 5, 39, 53, 65, 66, 125, 199, 201–203, 205, 206, 209
George, Lake, 78
Georgia, 133, 134, 145, 168, 170, 193
Georgia troops, 133, 134, 173
Germain, Lord George, 30, 65–67, 97, 99, 100, 109, 110, 199, 203–205, 207, 209
Grant, Maj. Gen. James, 42, 43
Grasse, Adm. François de, 196–98
Green Dragoons, 141, 144, 152, 160, 170, 173, 182
Green Mountain Boys, 10–13, 88, 90, 96, 159
Greene, Maj. Gen. Nathanael, 5, 40–42, 50–54, 114, 119, 120, 148, 165–69, 177, 179–89, 191–94
Guilford Courthouse, 180, 181

H

Hamilton, Col. Alexander, 62, 157
Hanoverians, 39
Head of Elk, 122
Heath, Maj. Gen. William, 198
Herrick, Col. Samuel, 90, 93
Heister, Maj. Gen. Philip, 42
Herkimer, Brig. Gen. Nicholas, 70–73
Hessians, 3, 39, 42, 51, 52, 56, 57, 61, 106, 139, 179, 182, 192, 198

Hillsboro, N.C., 147, 156

Howard, Col. John, 174, 175

Howe, Adm. Lord Richard, 38, 40, 57, 111, 126

Howe, Maj. Gen. Robert, 131

Howe, Gen. Sir William, 6, 22–28, 37, 38, 45–51, 53–58, 64–66, 98–100, 103, 104, 109–13, 115, 122–27, 198, 206

Hudson Highlands, 51, 198

Huger, Brig. Gen. Isaac, 140, 141, 167–69, 177, 178, 180, 181, 186

I

Indians, 67, 69, 70, 72–74, 76, 90, 92, 94, 100, 102

K

Kalb, Maj. Gen. Baron de, 3, 146–48, 152, 154, 155

Knox, Maj. Gen. Henry, 26, 59, 121

Knyphausen, Gen. Baron Wilhelm von, 139

Kosciuszko, Col. Thaddeus, 3, 101, 135, 167, 168

L

Lafayette, Marquis de, 121, 195, 196

Lancaster, Pa., 113, 127

Learned, Brig. Gen. Ebenezer, 105

Lee, Col. Henry, 167, 179, 182, 183, 188, 193

Lee's Legion, 179, 182, 183, 186, 188–90, 193

Lee, Maj. Gen. Charles, 30, 31, 54, 55, 129

Leslie, Maj. Gen. Alexander, 167, 178

Lincoln, Maj. Gen. Benjamin, 105, 133, 134, 136, 140–43, 147

Long Island, S.C., 31

Loring, Mrs. Joshua, 123, 124

M

Magaw, Col. Robert, 52

Manhattan campaign, 47–50

Marion, Col. Francis, 158–60, 167, 193

Martin, Josiah, 29, 30

Maryland troops, 46, 55, 146, 150, 152, 155, 173, 175, 187, 189, 191

Mass. Provincial Congress, 18

Mass. troops, 46, 92

Mathew, Maj. Gen. Edward, 136

McCrea, Jane, 82, 84–86, 97, 103, 145

Mifflin, Brig. Gen. Thomas, 59, 120

Miles, Col. Samuel, 43

Minute Men, 4

Mischianza, 125, 126

Mohawk River, 68, 69

Mohawk Valley expedition, 68–74

Montgomery, Brig. Gen. Richard, 208, 209

Morgan, Brig. Gen. Daniel, 4, 5, 78, 102, 105, 157, 167–75, 177–79, 182, 189, 208, 209

Morris, Robert, 59

Morristown, N.J., 64, 111

Moultrie, Gov. and Brig. Gen. William, 31, 34, 134

Mt. Hope, 78

Mt. Independence, 78

Murray, Mrs. Robert, 48

N

Navy, American, 3, 81, 140, 143
Navy, British, 2, 6, 28–38, 57, 67, 68, 78, 81, 111, 112, 115, 131, 136, 139, 198
Navy, French, 129, 130, 134, 196, 197
New Brunswick, N.J., 55
New Hampshire Grants, 8–10, 79, 87–89, 97
New Hampshire troops, 93
New Jersey troops, 55
New York City, 2, 45–47, 103, 111, 128, 131, 138
Newport, R.I., 128, 130, 131, 138
Ninety-Six, S.C., 145, 162, 168, 170, 193, 194
North Carolina troops, 133, 147, 150, 152, 154, 162, 172, 187, 189, 190
North Castle, N. Y., 51, 54, 55

O

Old Point Comfort, Va., 196

P

Pacolet River, 170
Parker, Adm. Sir Peter, 28–32, 34–36, 38, 129, 135
Partridge, Bellamy, 57
Pee Dee River, 149, 168
Pennsylvania troops, 43, 45, 55
Percy, Brig. Gen. Earl Hugh, 51, 52
Philadelphia, 113, 122, 123, 126–28
Phillips, Maj. Gen. William, 78
Pickens, Brig. Gen. Andrew, 159, 167, 172, 174, 175, 186, 193
Pitcairn, Maj. John, 21
Prevost, Maj. Gen. Augustine, 134, 135

Pulaski, Count Casimir, 135, 136, 140
Putnam, Maj. Gen. Israel, 42, 51, 52

Q

Quebec, 1, 208, 209

R

Rall, Col. Johann, 52
Ramsour's Mills, 178
Raritan River, 55
Rawdon, Col. Francis, 150, 152, 153, 193, 194
Reed, Brig. Gen. Joseph, 58
Regulators, 29
Resources, American, 1–4, 24–27, 31, 34, 45, 47, 48, 51, 59, 86, 89–91, 100, 104, 113, 114, 131, 133–35, 138, 140, 144, 146, 150, 152, 167–70, 180, 182, 185–87, 192, 197
Resources, British, 1–5, 21, 22, 24, 25, 27–29, 32, 36–39, 42, 43, 45, 51, 59, 67–69, 75, 88, 89, 101, 104, 111, 113, 131, 135, 136, 138–40, 144, 145, 150, 153, 167, 170, 174, 179, 180, 185–87, 192, 194, 196, 198, 209
Rhode Island, 55, 131
Rhode Island troops, 40, 119
Riedesel, Maj. Gen. Friedrich von, 79, 80, 87, 106
Rochambeau, Gen. Jean, 196
Rutledge, Gov. John, 31, 34, 134, 140

S

St. Clair, Maj. Gen. Arthur, 77–79, 87

St. Johns, Que., 68, 75
St. Leger, Lt. Col. Barry, 69–74
Salisbury, N.C., 180
Savannah, Ga., 134–36
Schuyler, Maj. Gen. Philip, 82, 83, 85, 86, 97
Skene, Capt. Philip, 11, 81, 82, 87–89
Skenesboro, N.Y., 8, 79, 81–83, 88
South Carolina troops, 133, 150, 162, 172
Sphinx, HMS, 35
Stark, Brig. Gen. John, 5, 89–95, 97
Stark, Molly, 94
Steuben, Lt. Gen. Baron Friedrich von, 121, 122, 146, 166, 187
Stevens, Brig. Gen. Edward, 152–54
Stewart, Lt. Col. Alexander, 194
Stirling, Maj. Gen. William, 43, 55
Sugar Loaf, 78, 80, 101
Sullivan, Maj. Gen. John, 43, 44, 112, 114, 130
Sumter, Brig. Gen. Thomas, 150, 159, 160, 167
Syren, HMS, 35

Tarleton, Lt. Col. Banastre, 140, 141, 144, 145, 152, 156, 158–60, 170, 173–77, 182, 183
Thayendanegea. *See* Brant
Throg's Neck, 50
Thunder, HMS, 33
Tories, 22, 24, 29, 30, 40, 69, 72, 87–89, 92, 93, 100, 102, 115, 123, 132, 144, 145, 159, 161, 163, 178, 185, 186, 202
Tryon, Gov. William, 29
Twiss, Lt., 78

Valley Forge, 115–26
Vermont. *See* New Hampshire Grants
Virginia, 136, 137, 145, 184, 194
Virginia troops, 144, 150, 154, 162, 167, 169, 173, 182, 185, 187, 190, 195

Waldeckers, 3, 39
Walloomsac River, 91, 92, 94
Ward, Maj. Gen. Artemas, 18
Warner, Col. Seth, 80, 90, 93, 94
Washington, Gen. George, 5, 18, 20, 25, 37, 39, 40, 44–56, 58–63, 79, 99, 100, 112–16, 119–21, 126, 129, 146, 148, 165, 195–97
Washington, Col. William, 175, 176, 182
West Point, 124, 194
Whigs, 202
Whitehall, N.Y. *See* Skenesboro
Whitemarsh, Pa., 116
Wilkinson, Brig. Gen. James, 121
Willett, Lt. Col. Marinus, 70, 72, 73
Williams, Col. Otho, 151, 153, 182, 183, 185, 186
Wilmington, N.C., 84, 193, 194
Winnsboro, S.C., 167

Yadkin River, 168, 180–82
York, Pa., 113, 127
Yost, Hon, 74